There Are No Pictures

An Autobiography

There Are No Pictures

An Autobiography

Virginia di Monda McCauley

Old Mountain Press

To purchase this book, order from our web page:
www.oldmp.com/nopictures.htm

Published by:
Old Mountain Press, Inc.
2542 S. Edgewater Dr.
Fayetteville, NC 28303

www.oldmountainpress.com

ISBN: 1-931575-57-6
Library of Congress Control Number: 2005926872

There Are No Pictures.

First Edition
Printed and bound in the United States of America by Morris Publishing • www.morrispublishing.com • 800-650-7888
1 2 3 4 5 6 7 8 9 10

This Book is Dedicated to

My Mother,
Lillian Alvino di Monda
and to
My Grandmother,
Teresa Amelia de Franco di Monda

Acknowledgments

I wish to thank my husband, Terry McCauley, my children: Diane, Brian, Amy, Terrence and Karen Slattery McCauley.

Annette Michael, who helped me to get my manuscript published.

Ann Spence, who recognized my need for a cathartic experience.

Bernadette Waite for your constant support and editing.

Carol Schutta, my life-long friend, who has always been there for me.

My grandson, Terrence James McCauley's pending arrival that forced me to live to write this autobiography.

Prologue

Love is a very mysterious thing – you never know who loves you and how much? You never knows who hates you and why they do? Somehow, I always knew I was different. Always, in the company of my grandmother. I have always loved her and she had always loved and cared for me, but I never knew how much.

My mother and I never had a good relationship, but I had my "Grandma" and it didn't make any difference with what was going on with my mother. When Grandma died a few months after I turned eleven, I was completely lost! I had no one, I had alienated my brothers for years, but they were forgiving and sympathetic. I had lost my confidante and my only true companion. I didn't understand everyone's reaction to me concerning Grandma's death. My father was never around, he was always burning the candle at both ends trying to make a not so successful taxi-cab business work. Now, I was faced with a mother, who I really didn't know, one who intensely loved me and I really didn't know how much of a sacrifice that love was. I was not an easy teenager to deal with. Again, I knew I was different, but I didn't know why.

During that eleventh year, I had dreams of being a prima ballerina, brain surgeon, veterinarian, nursery school teacher, beautician or an artist. Well, two out of six isn't so bad. I have worked diligently to achieve what I have never knowing how unique the challenges were that I faced. I had wanted to be loved again, I wanted someone to care for me and when she did, I didn't know it, or how to respond to it.

Life begins

It was a beautiful May morning; the air was filled with a warm gentle breeze. My heart was full and all my dreams were about to be fulfilled. I was getting married, I would now forever know the touch of his skin, the sweetness of his breath. I was going to be his and he would be mine forever. My childhood never foretold how my life was going to unfold. Terry's embrace was all I needed to sustain my zest for living. His passion was matched by no man on earth. My search was over, my life was just beginning.

Who am I? Am I Jacqueline Susann, Danielle Steele or Nora Roberts? Sorry, none of the above, I am Virginia di Monda McCauley.

This is truly the story of my life. Although you may not find it as enjoyable as the novels from the authors I just mentioned, neither did I. But for my own saving grace, I have to tell this tale. I have to tell my story, just to help me believe it myself.

In all actuality, my life started on my Wedding Day. May 1, 1965, I wasn't born that day, but that's when my reality started. In life you have to take the good with the bad and the good was Terry. And that goodness happened on the day I became Mrs. Terrence James McCauley. It was an absolutely glorious day in every sense of the word The skies were bright and crystal clear. The plans were made, the day was in motion. Onward and upward, I hoped and prayed.

I met Terry through my oldest brother Ceasar. They were both members of the volunteer fire department in North Merrick. The Jolly Volleys were a group of dedicated firemen. Back in those days, you didn't have to say fireperson to be politically correct. Women were practically a nonentity involved in the fire service. The drill team was a group of mentally disturbed firemen who would jump off the back of a modified speeding fire truck traveling fifty miles per hour. And this was fun?

"You have to be kidding!"

Yet every weekend, hundreds of people would watch this activity in the blistering sun for hours, just to see their favorite team. I never really appreciated their daring attempts to escape hospitalization; however, I did notice Terry at one of the tournaments. My brother always thought I should attend- God forbid his collegiate sister might become a spinster at age nineteen... Since I worked five days a week and went to school four evenings in Manhattan, I deliberately went to as many torturous weekend tournaments as possible, I made it through that summer without sun-poisoning or Terry, but I set my sight on him and I was hell-bent and determined.

Terry was and still is a very handsome man. As a young spirited hunk, just back from the Army joined the Fire Department as his father did before him. My catch had a wild Elvis Presley look, Elvis was my first idol, Terry was my only. I tried very hard to nab him, even traveling to unfamiliar areas. The last parade of the season was at <u>Rockaway Playland</u> in Far Rockaway, Queens, I drove in circles for hours , at one point I was driving in the middle of the parade. Ironically, Far Rockaway is where I now teach and such a lovely place it is (ha-ha). Terry never showed up that night and I got matched up with some dufus. But at the end of September, I went, with my brother's urging, to the dedication of the new Fire Hall. Terry was there, his current girlfriend was not. I'm not a drinker, but that day I really tied one on. Vodka was my new found friend. I was like a clothes line, everything in pants was hanging on me. I was so cockeyed drunk, I was half out of my mind. But guess who drove me home? And, gee, he already knew how to get there. Imagine that, I don't think I was the only one planning the Kismet. The next day, Monday, was I sorry! I was no longer happy! Boy, was I hung- over!

Frequently, I took my car to the Texaco station, where Terry worked part time and it was always during that shift that my car happened to need gas. To this day Terry still gases up my car, a chore that I abhor. I knew there was a Fire Department dance coming up on Thanksgiving Day weekend. I knew if I showed up at the Annual Children's Ragamuffin Parade on Thanksgiving morning, he would ask me to it. Besides, I had already bought the dress for the occasion and I went so far as borrowing a friend's kids so I would have a reason to be at the parade and, of course, according to my schedule, he complied.

My brother was having my niece, Susan's Christening, the day after the dance. On Saturday, the day of the first date, Ceasar asked me if he should invite Terry to the christening.

I told him "Wait, I want to see what happens at the dance. I don't want to be stuck with somebody at a family affair who may turn out to be a jerk."

Well, when I gave Caesar the nod he invited him and since my family was so large, Terry thought he was being inducted into the mafia. One cousin who didn't realize that the night before was our first date, asked him

"When are you two getting married?"

Terry shakily replied, "In a year and a half..."

He was so scared to give the wrong answer.

We did get engaged eleven months later.

Right around Christmas, before we were married, I was very sick. My mother called in a doctor for a house call; I couldn't even get out of bed. His diagnosis was extreme gastroenteritis. My good friend Barbara's wedding was in three weeks and I knew something was drastically wrong but I didn't want to upset her day and besides I was in the Bridal Party. I waited 'til the Monday after her big day and found I had a tumor on the ovary. The doctor said I could hold out for a few days before the surgery as I had four days before my finals in college. I went back to the surgeon for another check up three days later and he told me I had to check into the hospital immediately. I chose to go home, shave my legs, and take care of my final designs, before I told my father that I had to go. Unfortunately, there was at least six inches of new snow on the ground and it was still coming down. It took us hours to get there, when normally it would have been a twenty minute ride. I ended up in the hallway and the next day they sedated me for the surgery. As I was being wheeled into the operating room, a nurse yelled "Stop, don't touch her, she's not twenty-one and no one signed the parental consent form."

It was like a scene out of a daytime soap. The hospital looked at the year of birth, not the month. My family doctor was cursing up a storm and he had to call my father at home. My mother thought I was dead until she heard me screaming,

"Don't worry Mom, I'm still alive. They didn't operate yet."

It took a few more hours for my father to get there, as it had snowed all night. I often wondered why they weren't at the hospital for the operation. "*Click*"....

I was in the hospital for eight days. After all it was abdominal surgery. I was out of work for two months, and I messed up my college GPA and my graduation requirements.

When Terry and I were making the arrangements at Sacred Heart Church for the ceremony they insisted that I have a notarized letter from my father for permission to get married. Terry didn't need permission, just as my brother, Philip didn't need permission two years before.

My friends didn't need permission. We thought it was strange, but we followed the rules. *Click...*

I worked in a bakery on Sundays just to pay for some extras. Each Sunday, I would bring home tons of cake. You see I closed the bakery, and my mother froze the fruits of my labor, literally. My mother served all the cake after the church and before the reception, everyone came to my house. After all we lived right across the street and some people traveled a distance. Where else would they kill a couple of hours? The bakery is how they got me to my bridal shower, that and my sense of curiosity. You see my brother, Phil's mother-in-law worked in a bakery that was part of the chain I worked in and the phone would ring in two bakeries at once until someone answered it. Well, a few weeks before the wedding the phone was ringing and ringing. Finally I answered the phone, just in time to hear my brother talking to his mother-in-law about Terry's bachelor party and that I shouldn't know about it, because I would tell him, as I have such a big mouth, which of course I do. When I got home, we had a rip roaring argument. I was furious. Two hours later, Phil called me and said, "We just ran out of liquor."

He asked me to take two bottles of rye from the dining room cabinet and bring it to his in-laws. Guess what? They caught me. It was all a set up, they knew they could rely on my fury. Voil`a, it was my bridal shower.

Our afternoon reception was held in the fire hall which was built just two years earlier, I wasn't crazy about the fire house decor. After all this wasn't a theme wedding, and the parade trophies didn't add a romantic touch, but the price was right. My father and mother didn't have to pay a hall rental fee, because of my brother and Terry's membership. I really didn't want a morning wedding, but I couldn't have a mass in the afternoon, unless it was a Sunday, which I didn't care for. The solemnity of the mass was important to me as I was the only practicing Catholic in my family. My first planned date was in August; however, my mother didn't want to wear a brasolette in the summer heat. Well, much to everyone's surprise that May day set a record for high temperatures. We got married at ten AM, but the reception wasn't 'til one. Guess where everyone went for coffee and cake? After, all we lived right there. The hall was beautiful, for a Fire Hall and practically brand new, unfortunately it didn't have air-conditioning. We had two hundred and eighty six people at our reception. My father, Philip di Monda had eight brothers: My mother, Lillian Alvino had five sisters and two brothers; My father-in-law, Jimmy McCauley, had one brother and nine sisters and my mother-in-law, Susan McCaffrey McCauley was one of six, with two sisters and three brothers. You could see how the numbers added up quickly, for the caterer and the thermometer.

The caterer was Continental of Bellmore, the owners name was Merick. Coincidentally that is the name of our town, North Merrick. The meal was served family style, except to the bridal party, when Mr. Merick asked

Terry if he wanted a third portion, he replied, "No" but I said, "I wanted one." He said with a reproaching tone in his voice that I was the bride and shouldn't be eating this much. To this, with my voice on edge and not with the quiet demure bride like behavior I said, "My father is paying for this! Now bring me the food." I guess that was the start of my full figure, which I still maintain, not to mention my big mouth attitude.

The photographer was Bernie from Crown Photographers in Massapequa, he took my brother Phil's wedding pictures two years before. After my wedding, he took Carol's and then her brother, Chuck's. Bernie took tons of pictures that day; however, there were not too many pictures before that day, no digitals, just Kodak Brownies and not one pointed at me. There is only one of my First Holy Communion and Ceasar has that and one I have of myself and my two brothers at Ceasar's Boot Camp graduation in Fort Dix, NJ. I paid for two pictures for my high school year book. Terry has one copy, I don't know where the second one is. I was in several bridal parties of my friends and relatives, so I have some adult pictures. But actually there are no pictures of me so to speak of before my seventeenth birthday. My family never had school pictures taken of me and there are no baby pictures. There are plenty of pictures of my brothers, but you know how it goes when the last one comes along. You would think that someone would have thought that these were Kodak moments and just went *Click...*

From my bedroom window, I could see right into Kenneth-Michael Cleaner's. I asked Ken to iron my wedding dress and train, which he did a perfect job. The only problem was he didn't trust me to pick up the dress and he was dead right! I wouldn't let anyone answer the phone or door. He said the next morning,

"I knew you were going to pull this."

The poor man didn't sleep all night, but I did, Every time I wanted to check on the dress, I would just look out the window. The gown was a plain A-line summer satin dress with seed pearls adorning the embroidered bell sleeves. I wanted a mantilla veil, but everyone gave me grief over the peculiarity of it and the price was exorbitant. I ended up buying a pill box hat, very popular because it was the sixties and Jacqueline Kennedy was the style setter.

My father and I drove around the block in the limo. When I lit a cigarette and burned a hole in my veil, my father was pissed and didn't hesitate to tell me. So much for the special look. We lived diagonally across the street from Sacred Heart Church which I still attend every Sunday. My father told my mother to walk, he said it wasn't far and she couldn't go in the limo that was reserved for him and me plus Carol, and my flower girl, who was my five year old cousin Melanie. *Click...* The other attendants rode in another limo. My brothers were in the bridal party, They waited by the Club-50, a bar and grill on the opposite corner; I guess they were trying to relax. Nobody in my family was a big church goer, except me. Because of the formality of the morning mass, they had to wear formal tuxedos with tails; mind you the reception was in a fire station. How's that for an oxymoron? My oldest brother Ceasar was upset, especially when a neighborhood kid came up to him and asked if "he was a magician." He was mad, but kept his cool. When I heard, I laughed my ass off. But, guess what? I still have it and it's growing wider as each year goes by.

Carol Parker was my maid of honor and two years later I was her matron of honor. My brother Phil was Terry's best man, Ceasar was one of the ushers and Terry's little brother Jimmy was the ring-bearer; they are thirteen years apart. My mother wanted to wear a long dress, but my mother-in-law said it was not proper for a morning wedding. I told my mother to get the long dress any way, but she didn't have the spunk to go against tradition. I always had the mind-set that my way is the best way. But my mother was more of a compromiser than an antagonist. *Click...*

Several of my friends from childhood were there. I was excited to share the day with two special friends from early childhood, and several others from my teenage years. Mary Ann, who I met when I was thirteen, came to the wedding with her husband Ray. She thought I might need moral support during the part when they say, "Does anyone object?" She figured I was going to say "I do". but obviously I didn't. Whenever Terry and I had an argument, I would visit my old married friends Maryann and Ray. The closer to the date, the more visits Maryann and Ray would get. They were more nervous than Terry and I. Most of my friends were more neurotic and nuts than I was. Well, that day anyway.

Old Friends

One old friend, who was not present, was Marcia.
Marcia

Marcia was really strange or I guess you could say weird... She had funny habits and her family life was crap. When five year olds can figure out that you have lousy home life, it's a sad situation. The Innis family moved into a new brick, Cape Cod style home. The house was nice, but was nothing spectacular. My Uncle Eddie and Aunt Betty lived in the same style that was right next door to us. They really changed their home into a beauty. The Innises changed nothing. Marcia used to take weeds out of the yard and twist them between her fingers for hours, she was mesmerized by them.

She would call them "her diddle weeds."

Ernest, her fat obnoxious father would punish and chastise her for playing with the weeds. Marcia wasn't pretty; she had stringy, dirty blond hair. The boys used to say she was hit in the face with an "Ugly" stick. Old Ernie didn't think she was pretty; he would give her menial tasks and never would ask her pretty younger sisters to do anything. I guess she was the Cinderella of the fifties, but there was never a Prince Charming. Fat Ernest used to drive a red Triumph convertible. I still wonder how he got his fat body into that little sports car? The question is why would a T.V. repairman buy such a car? A man with a wife and three daughters? After he got his girth in there, there was no room for anyone else.

In fact, the only real Prince was my dog Prince, the rogue of the neighborhood. Prince, a roving mutt, hated Ernie, but he loved to bite the tires on the Triumph as the fat man drove by. Prince was an excellent judge of character for a mongrel. Merrick Avenue was the busiest street in town and it still is. My house was on the corner of Old Mill Road and Merrick Ave., As soon as Ernie made the turn, the dog would start his chase and all the kids would laugh, (Sometimes Marcia was laughing with us.)

Many times, as he was working on his, "Casper Milk Toast Tan" while smoking and reclining in the backyard, he looked like a beached whale. Ernest would make his oldest daughter pick up every match stick. No one was allowed to help her; we would just have to watch her humiliation. Ernest Innis was one of the most hateful men I ever met, he hated me and tried to hurt me in many ways. All of which I didn't understand until just a few years ago. *Click...*

When we were in the seventh grade, Marcia's grandmother died and Ernest received a large inheritance. They moved to the end of Old Mill Rd. The house was a brand new, split level and it cost seventeen thousand dollars. (I asked) It still didn't look that great in comparison to the others in that neighborhood. Three years later, Ernest moved his family to Huntington. That house wasn't new, and but was the best looking of all of his three houses. I guess plain old Merrick wasn't high fallutin' enough for him.

Marcia was a do nothing right kid, her father outwardly favored her two younger sisters. Her mother Doris, a tall, thin woman was very nice, but she didn't rule the roost like fat Ernest. A few months before my wedding Marcia came to my house with Carol and Dale. I was making a muslin copy of my wedding dress. Marcia wanted the four of us to go to a bar, and I begged off because of the sewing. I knew that Carol and Dale were stuck, but I couldn't help them. Marcia didn't come to my wedding. By that time she escaped to New Orleans to marry a chef named, and this is the truth, Peter Fucks. A few years later we learned Marcia was arrested for running a prostitution ring. I heard Marcia didn't live past her early thirties. Everything about her life was a sad story.

But Dale was there.

Dale

Dale moved into our neighborhood when we were six. She lived in the model ranch home on the corner of Gardenia and Old Mill Road. Dale's last name was Greenblat, but they later shorten it to Green, (which I found this to be amazing that if someone didn't like their name they could legally change it.) I wasn't too happy to have the last name diMonda, because of the unusual spelling, and the fact that it started with a lower case letter. Also, it wasn't a common name like

Parker or Green. Dale's father Ted was a draftsman of some type. I was always enthralled by artistic professions, even at young age. I knew my calling.

Dale's mom was the epitome of mother earth and a real life Jewish mom. Rae Green was one of the most caring women I have ever had the good fortune to meet. When we were little, Rae would make special quickie pie lunches for us. She would take two pieces of buttered bread, put all kinds of cheese and sandwich fixings in them. Then she would hold them over the stove burner carefully flipping them from side to side so as not to burn them. We had to eat them slowly or the cheese and hot tomatoes would burn our mouths and make them sting. Sometimes she would order Chinese food and we would eat on real china in their dining room. *Click...*

When we were in Junior High, we would hang out by some swimming streams that ran under the Southern State Parkway. There were about fifteen of us and we would build huts deep in the woods. You could be right next to one and never know it was hidden there. The hideouts lasted for a few summers and the cops couldn't even find them when the winter came and there were no leaves to shield them. They were complete shelters with couches and all the comforts of home; they were better than on *Survivor*. Many nights the boys would sleep in the woods .But there was never any sexual promiscuity going on. It was all good clean fun and friendship. You might find this hard to believe, but

I have many witnesses that can attest to the virtuous summers.

Carol hung out with Bobby and everyone was impressed that a Junior High student was going with a High School Junior. I really liked this guy named Cliff, but he really liked Dale and I was no competition for her, and, besides, she was one of my best friends. Years later I learned that Bobby, Carol's old boyfriend, entered the army with my husband, as his service buddy.

Dale was the oldest in her family and the only girl with two younger brothers, Wayne and Robbie. I guess this is why Carol, Dale and I bonded, more with each other than Marcia. To this day Carol, Dale and I try to get together at least once a year. We are all teachers. Carol and Dale work for private schools while I used to work for the Diocese of Brooklyn. In fact, Carol got me the job. Sally Parker, Carol's mom, told her that this move would break up our friendship. That was in 1986 and we still speak to each other on practically a daily basis. But I had to switch to the public school, because I couldn't afford to *Kiss IT UP TO GOD* anymore. Besides, Terry wanted to retire from the Railroad. and I need to get some better medical plans for us both. But Far Rockaway is another part of this story. Tune in several chapters ahead...

Back to the sixties...None of us left town for college. I went to FIT, The Fashion Institute of Technology, for textile design. Carol went to Farmingdale College for nursing; she stayed in the dorm originally then switched to Molloy in Rockville Center for education. Dale went to Hofstra for English Education. We were all heading off to different colleges, and we were going out into the world in different directions. It's ironic, the three of us ended up as teachers. We all live within a few miles of each other and live different life-styles.

Mary Ann

Mary Ann was a friend from my early teens. MaryAnn was the only child of Italian parents from Freeport. My brother and I belonged to a youth organization called the Allied Nautical Cadets it was a nautical answer to the Boy or Girl scouts. Philip was a very popular guy; he even ended up starting a fraternity with mostly Freeport High School friends. One of Phil's friends was Tommy Portale. Tommy's family still lives in a big house on the water in South Freeport. The house was so big that it became the center for most of the fraternity parties. Tommy would invite his younger cousin, Mary Ann. She was permitted to go because it was a family member's house. I was asked by Barry August to one of the parties I really wanted to go, but I ignored Barry all night. A year later he was my heart throb, but it wasn't a mutual feeling, then I was crushed...

Mary Ann and I became fast friends and still are to this day. There was a sorority that was trying to get off the ground, a girl, by the name of Betty Jean, also from the Nautical Cadets, asked me to join, so I went to a meeting in North Freeport. I wasn't fond of Betty, but I was interested in the sorority. The meeting was at a girl's house, her name was Beth, and she was the president of the group. I had so much to say that at the end of the meeting Beth's mother asked me to be the president. I gladly took over the job; my ego wouldn't allow me to do anything different. The sorority grew in leaps and bounds; I started recruiting my old friends from Merrick and new friends from Freeport. Mary Ann was one of the first. Sigma Phi Kappa became quite a large popular group. I still have the sweater.

My sweet sixteen was a surprise that Mary Ann organized. It was held in a very large bedroom of one of the members. The high light was when the party was crashed by the fraternity The following year was Mary Ann's turn, hers was a party at Jan Paz's house. I could still taste the cake her mother made: it was a peach shortcake, the size of a turkey platter. On special occasions when her mother knew I was coming, she would make it just for me.

Mary Ann is a year younger than I am. She was an excellent student and was set to go to secretarial school after high school graduation. Mr. and Mrs. Portale didn't really care for Mary Ann's boyfriend Ray, a kind of a wild guy, who lived next door. In fact, they were really on her case. Mary Ann and Ray went to an engagement party where they decided to elope. So off they went to Iowa, where one of Ray's sisters lived. Her parents put out an alarm covering numerous states, Iowa not included. The police were dragging the canals in Freeport. When they called and announced they were married in IA, I was at her home. I thought her mother was having a stroke, instead she was just passing out from the shock of Ray calling her "Mom". When they returned home, her mother and father had a church wedding and a garden reception. I wore a very tight white sheath dress. Mary Ann's aunt told me that she was going to let Mary Ann's young cousin wear her Communion dress, but felt it was in poor taste because the bride wore pale pink, since she had been married two weeks before. I left the reception and didn't tell my friend for years. This ill-fated couple that nobody thought would make it, celebrated their fortieth anniversary in July of 2003.

Carol

Carol was and still is my closest friend. She and I know each other's thoughts and feelings before they appear.

Sally

Mrs. Parker, Sally was always a working mother like my own; I guess that's why Carol and I were the closest of the four. Marcia and Dale had stay-at-home moms with younger children. Sally Parker worked as a babysitter 'til her late eighties. All the while she was still making her homemade jelly and jam from the grapes and raspberries in the backyard. When we were little, we would eat all kind of fruits and berries from the vines. Even though she worked, she was still a den mother for Chuck and a worker with the Girl Scouts for Carol. Her granddaughter, Margaret even roped her into the 4-H.

Mrs. Parker suffered a stroke early in January of 2003; sadly, she lasted until the end of September 04.

Charlie Parker was a very devoted father to his twins. He was a quiet man who thought of Carol and Chuck first. I remember that he made stilts of all different sizes and we would have a blast competing against each other in the driveway. When Carol and Chuck celebrated their mother's ninetieth birthday two years ago, out came the stilts and we were at it once more. Charlie was a member of the Elks club, and they were having a car raffle, so Charlie bought a few tickets, one for each member of his family. Carol's was the winning ticket. But guess what? So was the seller of the ticket. Great news, the Parker family won two brand new 1954 Buicks, one of which they sold, Sally didn't drive back then and Carol and Chuck were only ten years old.

Carol and I have different views and opinions, our phone conversations can go on for hours as each of us tries to get our point across. We had one physical altercation in our lives; we were about ten-it was winter. There was snow all over the ground and we were in Carol and Chuck's side yard. We all were bundled up wearing coats, snow pants, hats, and gloves I don't know what started the brawl, but I was clearly the aggressor and the victor. I guess that's why I remember it so clearly.

Charlie was an excellent wood-worker. He made lamps and chairs and put down all new floors in his house. This was his love, though not his actual job. He worked at La Guardia Airport as a plane mechanic, real blue collar worker. He was always the chauffeur, driving all of us to school parties and dances.

We had a Sadie Hawkins Day dance while we were in Junior High, (That's a dance where the girls invite the boys.) It's usually held on or around the 29th of February. I wanted to invite Cliff, but Dale beat me to it. I attended with my small group of friends. I asked my father to drive us, but he said he couldn't. He had to drive his cab that night. I ended up dancing with some nerdy kid named Kenny. He was someone to dance with, just so we both wouldn't be wallflowers. As we waited for Charlie Parker to pick us up, lo and behold, who should appear but my father? I was so excited. I yelled to Chuck and Carol to call their father and tell him that my father was there. But my dad told me he was there to pick up a passenger. Out comes fat, nerdy Kenny, who obviously was a frequent rider. *Click...* Charlie Parker drove us all home.

Carol's aunts, always played an important part of her life and they still do. Carol had a special kinship with her cousin Linda. Linda was a few years younger than us. Sadly, she passed away when she was just thirty-nine. Carol was devastated; we were on vacation during the wake and funeral. I felt guilty, I wasn't there for her. It kept happening every summer around Carol's daughter Margaret's birthday. Someone died and we were always away camping

When I would visit my grandfather at my Aunt Dolly's apartment and Carol visited the aunts' house we would both play in the same park in Brooklyn. Ironic, isn't it?

Elementary School

We all started at Camp Avenue School. My kindergarten teacher was Miss Mueller, Years later when my own children were in school, I worked with her on many committees. By then her name was Marshall and I didn't realize that Miss Mueller and Mrs. Marshall were one and the same.

When I was in second grade they opened a new school and we all were moved to the North School. Carol, Dale, Marcia and I were rarely in the same class. They had four tracks and most of the time we were split up for a few of the grades; I was with Chuck and Dale. I was a free spirit and my acquaintances changed often.

Jimmy Slattery

Jimmy Slattery was really the only boy I spoke to in grammar school besides Carol's twin brother Chuck. .Jimmy and I were in the same 5th and 6th grade classrooms and religion classes' Religion was on Wednesday afternoon and the Catholic students would be released early. Jimmy and I would walk together over the parkway bridge. There was stone wall ledge which was about four feet high, I would never walk on it, but Jimmy always would. He was more of a daredevil than most of us and he walked to a different beat.

When he did his tight rope walk on the wall, I was petrified for him.

One day he played a trick on me. I was always vulnerable to his games. He asked me, if I wanted a piece of <u>Bit Of Honey</u> candy. My answer was "Yes". Then he spit his candy into my mouth, it was repulsive and to this day I can't eat that candy .Jimmy was very feminine in Junior High and I know he was having a hard time. We all lost track of him about this time, until Carol saw a headline in one of the supermarket check-out line scandal sheets .She had read that Jimmy died in 1974. Jimmy Slattery had died in his thirties, at the time of his death, he was known as Candy Darling. Ironic as I always remember the candy incident with me that this should become his new identity. Candy Darling was a ground breaking force when it came to the first gender bending transvestites. He was a drag queen and he was also an Andy Warhol fixture. Andy Warhol, was the pop artist who painted Campbell Soup Cans and Marilyn Monroe florescent shadow face paintings. This is also ironic, since I am also a painter. The film called <u>Flesh</u> was his only real claim to fame. When Jimmy died, his family destroyed most of his private papers.

Jimmy Holsinger

Jimmy Holsinger was one of the most obnoxious kids you ever met. He was small and nerdy, thought he was God's gift, but he was just plain mean. He would make fun of me because I wasn't a spotless kid. He was hurtful to everyone, I never realized how many people didn't like him till we were older. My grandmother raised me and because of her advanced age, she never instilled in me the proper hygiene habits.

One day we were watching a film about "Pippy Long Stockings" he thought it would be humorous to tag me with the name "Piggy Lipshitz" He tried to hang this nomenclature on me for what seemed like an eternity. Fortunately, it didn't happen, but I always hated him and would never think of him in a positive way. He must have moved away from North Merrick because he never graduated with the rest of us from Calhoun. The most ironic part of this story is that my parents moved right next door to his house on Van Nostrand Ave. right after I got married

On the block a few houses past Carol and Chuck's there was this creepy guy (in his thirties) we used to call "Crazy Charlie". I used to cut through the woods behind his house to see my friends. Someone had put up a high bar between two trees, and being the tomboy I was, I would stop and do some flips or turns on the rust-coated bar. I often did this until suddenly Crazy Charley helped me down in a most inappropriate way. When he surprisingly grabbed me between my legs, I screamed even though no one heard. And I never went anywhere near him again. And I never told anyone this happened, I should have so the bastard could have been arrested. **Damn pervert!**

Dorothy Dankle

A few blocks over was Dotty Dankle's house. It was about a half of a mile from my house and since I was a wanderer, I used walk and ride all over the town. Dotty was in my kindergarten class and most of my classes in the elementary schools and quite a few in junior and senior high school. Just last year, Terry and I attended her wedding. She was always a character, fun loving, enjoying school, but always enjoying her friends more. Dotty wasn't a kid anymore, in fact she had three daughters of her own when she started to work diligently to change her career from chiropractor to operating room nurse at North Shore Hospital. Dotty says she may have some old class pictures from elementary school, but I don't even remember being there on picture day.

In the other direction, north of my house near the Uniondale line was where MaryAnn Jones and Carol Evans lived. They had common last names; they lived in new Cape Cod houses, very neat inside and out .I brought them into the sorority, Sigma Phi Kappa, where I was a charter member. I haven't seen them in years. But, when I'm in that area of town, I always think of them.

I was always a take charge person no matter what the situation. I always wanted to be top dog. Even at Far Rockaway High School, where I now teach Fine Arts, people refer to me as the pushy broad, a term I admire and am proud of.

I used to ride an old rusty boy's bike. It was probably a resurrection of Philip's. I rode this bike wherever I went which was generally all over the place. I was like a little vagabond traveling in any different direction on any given day. Most of the time nobody, including me, would know where I would end up that day. Some-times I was in ear shot of my name, but most of the time I was not. Many times I would just ignore the broken English of my elderly grandmother. Kids would just say *"Virginia"* your grandma's calling you. I think they were just trying to get rid of me. *Click...*

From as early my as memory allows my Grand-mother diMonda took care of me. Grandma was one of the greatest women in my life. She died when she was seventy-seven. I'm sure it was very difficult for her to take charge of me from infancy to when I became eleven She took me everyplace, we went all over town, and if the bus gave frequent miles traveled I would still be riding for free. The shopping area we went to was Hempstead. Grandma liked to go to the Fine Arts Theatre, I would have preferred going to the Disney movies across the street at the Calderon. But Grandma wanted to see her Italian movies, she understood Italian. I was too young to read the subtitles and I couldn't have cared less about them and it wasn't until years later that I realized that the movies were fine arts or by today's standards we would call them "Porno Flicks".

My brothers did not like grandma; she definitely favored me over them. I thought of myself as a seven year-old prima ballerina I would dance in front of the TV and block my brothers' view and when they com-plained it was always justified and they were sent away from the one and only television set. They called me a spoiled brat and I guess they were right. Grandma picked out all my clothes, I always had to wear skirts or dresses that weren't the *in thing* like the other girls wore. They were faggy and had a matronly look about them. When I was in the third grade she bought me some leather oxfords. She got a great deal during one of our trips to Brooklyn, so she bought me thirty pairs all red, and different sizes, I hated them, but that didn't make any difference. *Click...*

Fifth grade was no better, side zipper girl's jeans just came into fashion; I wanted a pair so bad I begged anyone who would listen. I kept saying all my friends had them and Merrick was always and still is a peer-pressure town. Marcia, Carol and Dale had them and I wanted them too. My mother brought me the jeans. My grandmother was so infuriated that my mother had bought me the pants that she cut them up. I saved the cut up jeans for months hoping they would miraculously repair themselves. I never got to wear them and when I told the kids at school that I had a pair, of course, nobody believed me because they never saw them. Then they started to call me a liar .But, I really had them... Really I did. *Click...*

In the early fall, in sixth grade, grandma took me for a hair cut. My scalp was terribly itchy and I couldn't stop scratching The beautician refused to cut my hair I had lice. I was devastated. The very next day the school nurse came into the classroom with an assistant they were checking everyone's head. I sat in the row next to the windows that was the last group to be checked. I was trapped. I could go to the bathroom and hide. But then I realized that wasn't going to work when some other kid tried that, they checked him before he left. I truly believe in the power of prayer. I prayed the whole time knowing exactly what they were going to find. I couldn't escape; I was getting sick to my stomach. Finally, I was called up for the head examination. I was ready to sink through the floor. When the ordeal was over, the infested had to report to the nurse's office .To my surprise, half of the class was called down. I was finally grouped with the popular kids. I was in with the in crowd. Grandma used a fine tooth comb and agonizingly cut out every nit. No more bugs. No more bond with the cool kids.

In high school, I was involved in sports and art. In my senior year, I designed the program for sports night. Mr. Robert Reeves was my art teacher, a man who changed my life forever. Now, I strive to be the same influential art teacher to my students, as he was to me. In my junior year, he took us on a field trip to FIT, the Fashion Institute of Technology. I was enthralled with the school especially with its Textile Design Program. I asked my father for forty dollars to apply to a few colleges The application fee for each school was $10.00.

He said,"Which one do you want to go to?"

I said,"FIT"

He replied "Well, since you can only go to one school at a time, pick one."

So I only applied to one college, in fact, I went for early admission. When I was accepted I was so excited, I hardly read the acceptance letter. I was waiting for someone from the art group to be going to college with me. Then someone finally told me they were also going.

Then she said" That they wanted the fifty dollars awfully fast."

"What fifty dollars?" I said

She told me I needed to hold my placement, especially because I went for early admission. I went home and reread the letter; sure enough I had to send the money. It was due months before. My father immediately sent the money. A few days before graduation I received my money back, my place was given to someone else. I was devastated I couldn't stop crying. I was only permitted to apply to one school and now I wasn't going anywhere.

I went to my Guidance Counselor, Mr. John Jordan. I couldn't control my tears. His compassionate response was that "Anyone that is this stupid doesn't deserve to go to college."

I said, "Drop dead" on my way out of the office. I felt guilty when the man suffered a heart attack and dropped dead a few years later.

I went to Mr. Reeves. He made some calls, then he drove me to the train station, paid for my ticket, and sent me to FIT that very same day. The school told me that I could go to evening school in the summer and the fall and that if I maintained a 4.0 average they would place me in the daytime program.

I started my college career the day after graduation. I fulfilled my part of the agreement. When the time came for me to move to the daytime classes I refused. I was carrying a full schedule at night and working a full time job in A.Seigel and Company, a paint store in Freeport, where I was the wallpaper consultant. I wasn't going to give up the job to go to school and earn the same amount of credits.

The September after my high school graduation, I was scheduled to take my driving test. For a short period in New York State's Motor Vehicle Codes you were only allowed to practice with a professional driving instructor. My luck, that period of time was when I was learning. I had no practice since the previous June before I graduated. It had been three months since I had been behind the wheel of a car. The day before the test my father was trying to figure out which car I was going to take my test in. I went from Uncle Marty's big Buick to Uncle Eddie's stick shift sedan. Finally, I ended up in one of my father's checker cabs. My practice on the car was in the teeming rain. My father kept yelling at me to watch the road.

I said, "I am."

But my head was swinging back and forth. Instead of watching the road, I was watching the windshield wipers. Duh. When we reached the test site in Freeport, the inspector started to argue with my father that I could not take the test in a commercial vechiele. My father countered back that the name of the company was <u>di Monda Brothers Taxi Inc.</u> and since I was a diMonda, therefore I was an owner and it was not a commercial vehicle in my circumstance. The inspector gave up and let me take the test. Needless to say, I was quite nervous and upset. When he asked me to parallel park on a major roadway, I quietly asked him to wait 'til the traffic light changed behind me. After waiting for a few seconds the inspector barked at me that he said for me to park. This prompted me to scream back, that I said "to wait." He immediately terminated the test. Two weeks later, I got my license in the mail.

I bought Ceasar's old car, my first, a 1956 Pontiac Bonneville convertible.

After a few semesters of night school, someone suggested that I go to the job placement at the school. They sent me to Cohn Hall Marx, a big ladies' blouse ware textile house. I went for an all day interview only to find out I didn't get the job. I went back to personnel to tell them off, they didn't need to take the whole day not to hire me. They called the stylist, Irene Speilberg, to find out what happened .She stated that she didn't want me, because I was too shy and quiet. The personnel manager told her "You should see her now" and of my behavior in his office. Guess what? I was hired immediately.

Imagine someone thinking I was quiet and shy.

Ha-Ha

Grandma and Grandpa di Monda

There was never any outward show of affection in my family, no one ever kissed in front of others, and I don't remember being held or coddled, even at a young age. The only time I can recall my hand being held was when someone was crossing me across a busy street.

When it came time for someone to speak to me about the facts of life, there wasn't anybody. Dale told me what she had been told by her mother, she showed me the book about the menstruation and periods, that was going to happen to me too. I was so stymied that I told all my cousins, Johnny and Bobby, who were nine, Carol who was seven and Deanna who was five. I didn't know that this is not what a young lady who was growing up should be discussing. Man, were my aunts and uncles furious with me .But, maybe someone should have taken time with me. *Click...* Even as a teenager, I was not happy when a regular party would end up as a make out party, it was a very uncomfortable situation. I lacked self esteem and I didn't feel good about myself. I never felt that I was attractive. I know now that this is typical behavior. But, then, it made me very uncomfortable.

Grandma used to crochet like a machine, she had such a fine hand. She would make beautiful tablecloths, scarves for the buffet and dozens of character dolls for me .The dolls were figures from stories like Little Red Riding Hood ,Cinderella, Snow White and all the bride dresses you could imagine. I had dolls from all different countries, there was so many and I couldn't count them. And now I couldn't tell you where one is. All the dolls and linens were supposed to be mine, but things didn't work out that way and I don't know why. *Click...*

But grandma said she always would take care of me; even if she were to die, she would still take care of me. When she kept telling me this over and over, I would cry.

I can't get these conversations out of my memories, they are so vivid in my mind. Grandma and me would sit on the bench behind Old Mill Road School. I didn't want to hear it, when

Grandma said,"I would get her money, just me and no one else."

I didn't want to be different from my brothers and cousins, I didn't want to be the object of anyone's hate or dislike. I was so afraid that I would be left alone, all I had was grandma I hardly knew my parents even though I lived in the same house as them. *Click...*

We lived in a great big house on the corner of Old Mill Road and Merrick Avenue. The house had some parts that were over a hundred years old .It was in the early forties when my grandparents bought the house. The property was approximately forty acres. My grandmother was a shrewd business woman; she kept buying and selling land. She sold seventeen acres to a new builder. My Uncle Eddie bought a house from the builder Mandell; Marcia's family also bought one of the brick capes in that group. Then my grandmother sold the second piece. Those houses are now known as Briarcliff Homes. Close friends of ours, Dick and Gail, with their daughter, Alexis live in Briarcliff. Terry and Dick are as close as brothers. We love them very much and treasure their friendship. I just recently learned that my cousin Bobby's daughter, Kari bought a house across the street from Dick and Gail. My grandparents believed that property was the root of all wealth. If my grandmother was free to purchase what she desired, I and all of my relatives would be "Dirt Rich". She wanted to buy half of the town's waterfront property, she wanted to buy the biggest restaurant on Merrick Road. She wanted my Uncle Robbie, Bobby's father, to check out some acreage in Saratoga, while he was on his honeymoon. She heard they were going to build a race-track near there and she thought it would be a good investment, but one of her older sons told her not to bother Robbie and Sophie. Since she had no way to go there herself, that idea was a photo finish that fell short by a nose of crossing the finish line.

My grandfather was a very dapper man. Photos show him wearing spats {shoe coverings to hide the laces}. If he was outside, he always wore a straw hat so he could tend to his many flower gardens and fruit trees. Typically, we had fig trees, after all we were

Italian. The hat was worn when grandpa painted the most gorgeous landscapes. He owned the land, tended it and painted it. I don't have any of his paintings, but many of my cousins do, they got them from their fathers. My father got none but he inherited many of my grandfather's undesirable traits. *Click...* I inherited the love of gardening and the desire to paint. My father inherited the love of women. Several of my cousins are also professional artists, as John, who passed away in the early nineties. Johnny was a very successful interior decorator, featured several times in the magazine <u>Architectural Digest</u>. Diane is a painter, Deanna works with stained glass and Bobby is a graphic artist. As for me, I paint and teach Fine Arts for the New York City Department of Education and I am also an adjunct for York College.

I think grandpa was a frustrated farmer, we even had a goat. Angelina was the nastiest animal you could ever imagine, she lived in our barn and you couldn't go anywhere near it. I wasn't even in school yet and she would scare the hell out of me so much that I wouldn't go outside.

Grandpa suffered a stroke in the early fifties, we had to be really quiet, and for me that was a difficult chore. I have never been and am still not a quiet person. Philip was in the forth grade and had just started to play the trumpet in the school band. He had to practice in one of the way too many cars abandoned in the yard.

Grandpa died in 1952.

But grandma, although her English was quite limited, was extremely intelligent and she was the brains behind everything. She was a mathematical wiz, she could do battle with the best of the best.

Unfortunately, she always appeased her nine sons and placated their wishes, while cleaning up their messes and mistakes. The one, who was more of a thorn in her heart, was my father, always a charmer who could talk his way out of a paper bag, while selling you the Brooklyn Bridge. Out of all of his brothers, he was the poorest. He and my mother didn't buy their only house until after I was married. I always thought grandma lived with us, but it was the other way around.

I was in the total care of my grandmother. It must have been very tough for a woman in her seventies to keep up with a headstrong tomboy. I did what I wanted, I was unsupervised most of the time. My hygiene was lacking completely and I didn't even know it. One time my Uncle Rudy and Aunt Irene came over and they kept telling me to go inside and wash the ring off my neck. I didn't know what to do. I kept looking for a little round spot, but I couldn't find it. Finally, my aunt took me into the bathroom and scrubbed it off; my teacher complimented me the next day. I was so grateful to my Aunt Irene, I asked her to be my confirmation sponsor and I even took her name as my middle name. This was really odd because Aunt Irene and Uncle Rudy were the relatives that I had the least contact with.

Their son, Richard, was the only cousin that I, rarely saw.

My uncles were all very attentive to their mother. There wasn't a week that went by without them all coming to see her. Uncle Ed was next door, Uncle Robbie and Uncle Marty co-owned a house in Roosevelt. Uncle Pressy lived in Roosevelt too. Uncle Charlie and Uncle Julie lived in West Hempstead, Uncle Rudy, was in Valley Stream and the oldest, Uncle John lived in Brooklyn, all within thirty miles. On Sundays, they would all gather for the macaroni dinner at their Momma's house. I had a slew of cousins .The younger brothers' kids were the closest, we hung out together, we socialized and some of us are close to this very day.

My Uncles Pressy and Marty had a roofing business. My father had a taxi-cab company. My Uncles Rudy and Charlie had a blouse factory. Most of these enterprises employed all the brothers at one time or another. The blouse factory was the only business that was partially successful. My father was the last to leave home in fact my grandparents were long gone before my parents left the old house and that was six months after I got married. *Click...*

The blouse factory was in Merrick village, now the building is home to Northeast Metal Products. The name of the company was "Maybelle Blouses" several years later, the company changed their name to "Topper Casuals" and moved to Elmont, a town on the Nassau – Queens line, not far from Belmont Race Track. Ironically, these were the two sons who talked my grandmother out of the Saratoga land deal. When they were in Merrick, grandma used to take me to the "shop". I was a child and I effortlessly mounted the three flights of steps to the top floor. Grandma, however, would struggle to the factory. Once, there I would run around, play with the thin cardboard boxes, go to the dumb waiter elevators on the floor and race around my uncles, who were embroiderers and the cutters.

I was the biggest pain in the ass, but they had to put up with me because I was grandma's favorite grandchild.

I could do no wrong.

The only one happy to see me was my mother. *Click...*

Mom

My mother was a presser. She would use a flat iron, powered by steam, and press an endless supply of blouses in a day. One time she made a deal with my Uncle Charlie; she was to be paid by the blouse, rather than a flat salary. Well, after a few weeks, when she was ironing a couple of hundred blouses in one day, my Uncle Charlie found this agreement was not lucrative to him and he reverted back to the old way (or my mother would be out of a job.) She had no choice; my father was not making a fortune at the cabs. She was only left with the pride, that she "beat" the brothers.

Sometimes my mother would take my brother Philip and me to the Mary Bill diner. Terry and I still go to this eatery, now owned by Mary and Nick. Mary is the original Mary's niece. Philip and I used to love sitting on the stools spinning at the counter, mesmerized by Bill cooking as fast as he could.

My mother never drove so when we went any place it was always by bus. You would have never known my father was a cab driver!

When I first started attending Merrick Ave. Junior High School, I wasn't in classes with my familiar neighborhood friends; I was involved in a whole new group, a group that I was trying to keep up with. The rage was to wear these neckerchiefs; they were square scarves made of very flimsy material. I didn't have the money to buy any, so I stole one 29 cent scarf from the local five and ten cent store called Germain's. I walked the two miles back home. A few hours later, my mother invited me to go shopping with her. I was really excited.

This was the only time I could remember going shopping with my mother. We rode the bus for the ten minute ride and went back into Germain's. Imagine my surprise when the manager approached us and my mother removed the scarf from her purse. She told me, "Why don't you explain how you got this?" She then paid the 29 cents, gave the man back the scarf, and we left for the bus stop. The ride back took "29 hours." When we finally reached home, my mother discussed the incident with me by using the wooden spoon.

My mother and I never had a close relationship. I was grandma's granddaughter, not my mother's daughter. But what mother has a great relationship with a teenage girl? When she said "black," my father would say "white," and I would say "gray". I marched to my own drummer. No one could tell me otherwise. When I got older, my mother and I would deliberately set up my father, so I could get something he didn't think was a good idea. Thanks, Mom!

My mother was a phenomenal cook. Her meatballs and sauce could be matched by no one. She could make a feast out of crappy meat and leftovers. She catered all the food for my mother-in-law's wedding to Nick.

Nobody liked Nick. Terry was not even sure if his mother liked him.

Daddy

He was a hard-working man; he worked eighteen hours a day and spent very little time at home. *Click…* When I was born, at the end of World War II, he worked for Bethlehem Steel. Soot and grime covered his skin and he drew the nickname, "Blackie." Most people referred to him by this name until the day he died. I hated this name as I felt it implied that some one was not clean, and I was already dealing with hygiene problems of my own.

One day I asked him, "Daddy, how come you named me Virginia?"

He said, "I was at the movies the night you were born and the actress starring in the film was *Virginia Mayo." *Click...*

*Virginia Mayo died on January 18, 2005 Age 84.

Virginia means "Virgin," diMonda means "of the world." I went through a third of my life with a name meaning, "Virgin of the World" and the initials VD.

Well back to Dad…I vaguely remember when he worked painting greenhouses. According to my brother, Ceasar, my father made a great deal of money at this profession. Sadly, he squanded the money on gambling and women. *Click...* Then he worked as a furniture mover, he was like a bull, and by far the strongest in his family. At times, he worked in the roofing business or the blouse factory.

In the mid fifties, his career started as a cab driver, working as part of a small fleet in Freeport. His desire was to have his own fleet of cabs. To accomplish his dream, he started out with one cab at the Freeport Railroad Station. After a short time, he rented a small storefront where he put his phone.

During the summer of my fourteenth year, I worked as the only dispatcher. I would receive three or four calls a day. When I got a call, I would lock up the office and run, as fast as I could, the two blocks to the Railroad Station to tell my father. I was left to walk back unless my father's pick-up was on the way. In that case, I hitched a ride from him.

The Texas Ranger hamburger shop next door to the office had a little trap door in the wall, connecting one business to the other. I didn't get paid money for my dispatching and running, but I got the most famous hamburgers on the South Shore of Long Island. My father came out on the losing end of that deal, those three or four fares were no match for my voracious appetite.

I had a lot of free time on this job, I met the shoemaker's daughter, Margie(her father ran a business two doors away from my father's) Her father Teddy did a fantastic business. I had no idea why people needed so much shoe repair until I was told years later that Teddy was my father's personal advisor concerning the horse flesh at Belmont (the guy was the town's bookie.)

Margie blocked men's hats, then she cleaned and shaped them. She was a year older than I, but Margie made a real salary. Now she only did a few hats a day. I wondered how it was possible that she made so much money and could shop in <u>Ruby Lane's.</u>

Ruby Lane's was a chain of women's apparel. It was matronly, but very convenient and affordable for most.

Eventually, business picked up, and the phone number really took off. My brother, Philip picked the number, 868-8888. He thought, and rightly so, that the number would be easy to remember. I thought it was a pain in the ass. We didn't have touch tones then and all those eights were a workout on a dial phone. When you have a phone that is used for just answering, one without a dial plate, the telephone company insisted that you have a dial able phone available so they, too, could make their profit.

My father now had two cabs and a radio system in which to contact the cars on the road. Also, he was moving into another storefront a few blocks away. He moved out, however, a month before the new office was ready, so he had to move the radio dispatching system and the phones into our kitchen on Merrick Ave. The incessant squawking and telephone ringing became nerve wracking but it was what paid some of the bills, some of the time. We had no choice. My mother became the primary dispatcher until the business was sold in 1976.

While I was dating Terry, I had to call him for some reason. My father said I had to use the pay phone. I always got on the phone with a hand full of change. Well, during our conversation, the operator cut in and said,

"Please deposit one nickel for an additional five minutes or the call will be interrupted."

I immediately deposited the money.

Terry said, "I thought you were calling from home"

I answered, "I was, we have a pay phone in our kitchen cabinet"

Terry raced over as fast as his 1960 Chevy Impala could get him there, just to see the phone. We had the phone for years, the phone company never came to empty the machine. That was a job for my father whenever the coin box got too full.

The bill collectors were always the wolves at the door. My uncles came to our rescue constantly. If my father needed five hundred dollars for an insurance bond or to repair the oil burner or just for fuel to heat the house, each one of the eight would show up with money to help us. The brothers were always our safety net.

My father was the Ralph Kramden of the sixties. He always tried hard to keep his head above water. One time he brought home six ducks;, he was going to breed them. They were cute, but they stunk. One of them had an injured foot. I guess you could call him a "Lame Duck."

Ha-Ha. After a year of quacking and no ducklings, Dad got rid of the ducks, I never wanted to know what happened to them. I shudder to think of our pets on someone's dinner plate. After the ducks, our father turned his attention to canaries and parakeets. We had gigantic cages mounted on the kitchenette wall and separate cages all over the house. There were feathers and bird droppings everywhere. Now the house stunk like the backyard, and I don't think he sold a single bird. My mother ended up with a canary that she had for years. The bird was a warbler which meant it could sing beautifully, and it lived for a long time. This bird moved to it's new home on Van Nostrand. His name was "Bird," twelve years old and the sole survivor of hundreds before him. You would have thought that he would have been named. But my mother loved him and hung his cage over the kitchen sink in front of a window.

Daddy's cab company kept growing. At one time he had six cabs going night and day. His most reliable driver was my father-in-law, Jim McCauley. He wouldn't let anyone touch his cab. When he wasn't working, neither was the car. Terry's Uncle Tommy was also a driver. Everyone loved him: he wasn't dependable, but nobody could ever say a bad thing about Uncle Tommy. Tommy was my mother-in-law's younger brother, and Susie, Terry's mother, worked there too. She tried to be the bookkeeper of my father's business. The books were the most convoluted system possible. The fights and arguments that would ensue were horrendous. The battle of the Garlic and the Gaelic continued for years, but it brought both families together.

When his five or six cars needed to be inspected, Dad had the one cab that my father-in-law drove: that was the *crème de la crème* of the fleet. My dad would bring the beauty for inspection; naturally, it passed. My Uncle Eddie was ready with a paint brush in hand, to change the cab number on the fender while my father was busy switching the VIN number. This process was repeated all day, and my father was safe for another six months. Eventually, The Village of Freeport caught up with him and they started asking him to bring the whole fleet in at once.

My father was a con artist; he was a smooth talking Joe Schmoe who was just trying to get ahead. One time, when Terry and I were selling an old Buick, he convinced the perspective buyer that the only thing wrong with the car was that it was missing the U in the word Buick. Of course, I wasn't allowed to talk during this transaction. It was like when he would pay his bills, and not sign the checks. When the bill collectors called, he would pretend that it was my mother's fault. It would buy him some more time to come up with the money.

What goes around comes around. He had this account with a Lutheran Church in Freeport; he would pick up their senior parishioners and the minister would pay him on a monthly basis. Well, guess what? One month the check arrived with no signature. We all laughed, but my father didn't think it was funny. He really needed the money.

Early Memories

The first memory I have of a doctor was Dr. Meili. My mother took me to him when I was old enough to know the pain, but young enough not to know how old I was. I had a very large boil on my rump and it had to be lanced. I still have the scar to prove it; unfortunately, I really can't turn around to see it without getting excruciating "fat" cramps. So much for my ass problems.

After that medical procedure, grandma used to take me to a Brooklyn doctor by the name of Ceravello. I remember the wait was always very long and we would take two buses and the el train.

Dr. Ceravello had a big wrap around porch around his house, but we would have to wait in the vestibule for him. The trip was so long and I just hated going and having to wait at the El (elevated train station) to go home. It felt so high in the air; with all those steps grandma was so winded that I was afraid for her, and I was afraid to wait for the noisy train on the narrow track that looked like it was about to fall into the street below. Why was I at a doctor in Brooklyn? *Click...*

Our backyard was not welltended, the weeds grew higher than the flowers, but we had roses. Boy, did we have roses. Roses that grew all along the back fence. The fence was in shambles as was our house. I think the roses were the only thing holding up the fence. If you could find flowers and buds that the aphids didn't get to first, you would have a beautiful bouquet of all different colors: red, pink, yellow, and white. And under the shade of the dogwood tree, we had hundreds of violets and lilies of the valleys. Each spring I would bring in big bouquets of roses and little handfuls of the tiny flowers wrapped in a napkin to my teacher. I believe the flowers were what got me decent grades. Teachers love presents, I should know–I am one.

Every summer I attended a recreation program at Camp Avenue School. I loved the arts and crafts program, I didn't like when we would have to rest after lunch. I was too hyper to just relax; it was painful for me to wait out the allotted time. The school was about three quarters of a mile from my house. I used to walk on the west side of Merrick Ave. where you could see the back of the Briarcliff houses. Once in a while I walked on the East side where there were a few houses spread apart by wooded areas. One very warm day, I found myself in trouble; a man in the woods suggested that I remove my blouse and undershirt. I ran as fast as I could. I didn't go back to the program ever again.

When I was in the fourth grade, the Art teacher named Virginia Lucas formed an Art Club. I didn't know you had to sign up or be picked to participate in it. I just found myself in it, and I loved spending my lunch period, once a week, making all kinds of wonderful projects in an overgrown custodial storage closet.

Aside from the arts, I was also very athletic. That came from me trying to copy everything my brothers did.

I was in the sixth grade in school. My grandmother had just died in January. I was still reeling from the grief but I didn't know it. A girl named Carol Stimemetz had a broken leg. I remember how she had that big clunky cast that people wrote on. A few months later, my class was playing dodge ball in gym. Someone threw the ball at me and caught me in my right ankle. I remember the pain was so excruciating that I could hardly move. I was sent home and rested a few days before I returned to school. This time, there was no doctor. *Click...*

Twenty years later, while I was dancing to "At the Hop" at a Fire Department dance with friend, Gail Kmitis, I broke my leg, only the doctor said it was a re-break. My mother remembered the incident; I remembered the pain and I walked around for twenty years on an unattended broken ankle. *Click...*

Crises in the Family

Three months before Diane was born, my parents were supposed to move into a house on Van Nostrand Ave. about six blocks from where they lived on Merrick Ave. My father didn't want to leave. It was quite a sad day.

Daddy was very thick headed and wasn't going to leave the house he lived in for twenty five years. My father was a diabetic and couldn't take the stress of moving. However, the property was sold and they had to go.

On a very cold January afternoon, just a few days before the move, my sister-in-law, Carol and I went shopping for a bed for my niece Judy. Her crib was needed for her baby brother or sister, due any second. When we arrived at my mother's house, Mom started yelling and screaming. You could smell the sense of fear in her voice.

"Raymond is hurt– Raymond is hurt." Raymond was Caesar and Joyce's nine month old baby. He was in his walker and while his mother was preparing dinner, he pulled the cord of the deep fat frying pan.The burning hot oil was 450*. It fell directly on his head, face and neck. It was the most horrendous accident one family could bear. He looked like something from a horror movie. The only ones who could bear to look at him were his mother and me. He still bears the scars thirty-eight years later. He suffered first, second and third degree burns. The poor infant was taken by the Fire Department ambulance to South Nassau Hospital in Oceanside. The next day Joyce was very sick and I had an obstetrician appointment so I took her with me. She used the same doctor so there was no problem. My appointment went fine, but the OB came out and told me to get her to a hospital that she was having a miscarriage. Again I was in charge; I called my brother who was home with his two year old daughter, Susan. I told the doctor I was taking Joyce to South Nassau to make it easier on the family. Now I was the only one who could go into Raymond's room. Joyce wasn't allowed to leave the floor she was on. The nurses thought I was his mother and I was very pregnant; they had a lot of compassion for our family. I would sing to my only nephew who was so badly burned that the doctors placed both of his little arms in plaster casts, so he couldn't bend his elbows or touch his deep burns.

The very next day my cousin Bobby's friends from Roosevelt Fire Department came to make the move for my mother and father. My dad wouldn't leave. It was so heart-rending to leave a home where he spent so little time with his family, yet he refused to go. Everything was moved around him. They just left him, his chair and the T.V. Finally he had to go to the bathroom and that's when the move was finalized. Daddy was in pain as unbearable as Raymond's. I got a call the very next morning from my mother; my dad was going into a diabetic coma. Again I transported him to South Nassau Hospital. That night Philip needed to borrow my big red Oldsmobile. The next day Carol went to a different hospital and gave birth to my second nephew, Andrew. Five people all with the same last name; this confused the hell out of the doctors and the hospital services as well as the rest of the family. Meanwhile, my mother and I just continued to move her in any way we could. We used garbage cans, drawers, and boxes. I was seven months pregnant, but I was the only one emotionally stable enough to handle this **family crisis.**

I drove my mother everyday to South Nassau Hospital to see my father, Raymond, and Joyce. One evening, I said to my mother:

"Come on, we're going to see something good tonight."

We drove to Freeport's Doctor's Hospital to see her newest grandson, Andrew.

Diane

Diane was born just three weeks short of our first anniversary; this was to stop all the old biddies and prudes from counting on their fingers. In those days that was an outward gesture meant to embarrass the woman, not the man. Diane was due three weeks before she actually arrived; at that time you didn't know or couldn't find out the sex of the baby.

The pregnancy was a terrible one. I was sick from day one and I would upchuck with out any notice. One day I borrowed my brother, Philip's car and I threw up down the window well. There was no way to clean it up entirely. A short time later, Phil got rid of the car; he couldn't stand the odor or the residue. I found the whole incident very funny.

Because I was constantly sick and not a great house-keeper, Terry said, "Don't bother to clean up the apartment. I'll bring my mother to clean up, while you're in the hospital." While I knew she would and never utter an unkind word about her slob of a daughter-in-law and that she was a meticulous house keeper, I still didn't want her cleaning the things I should have been taking care of all year.

Terry's birthday is the 19th of April. The week before that, on the 12th, I was at my mother's all day.

She lived right around the corner from me. I felt terrible, my back was killing me. My mother suggested that Terry take me to the doctor's office in Levittown. Dr. Gardner told me I wasn't going to have the baby for weeks, that she wasn't in position. We were right across the turnpike from May's Department store and since we weren't going to have the baby for a while, we decided to go shopping for Terry's birthday gift. My mother didn't know what had happened to us until we arrived back much later, packages in hand. When we got home about nine pm, I was really in agony. I distracted myself by starting to clean. At one point I went to the bathroom, for a much needed water call. After washing woodwork until two in the morning, I finally had to resort to calling the OB. His response was to go to the hospital, and he'll take care of the not so urgent matter in the morning. I told Terry I didn't want to go, that I was embarrassed The doctor intimated that I was being foolish. The next thing I knew, Terry called his mom not to clean, but to come with us.

As bad as the pregnancy was, the delivery was worse. I didn't know that my urgent bathroom call was in reality my water breaking. I was given a lot of drugs; that's how you delivered in those days, with just a slight memory of what was happening to you. Six hours after we arrived at the hospital, I gave birth. One doctor went down to tell Terry that I was allright. He wasn't even sure of the sex of the baby. He was concerned that it was a difficult birth, but both mother and child were going to be allright. Diane was a rear-end breach; she never was in the proper position. The other doctor went down to Terry and his mom and told them it was a girl. My mother-in- law was delighted. After two sons, there was finally a little girl. The doctor told Terry to go home, get some rest, and then rise make some calls, and come back to the hospital in about five hours. After all, with all those drugs, I wasn't going to be awake.

However, I did wake up very quickly and the hospital allowed my mother and sister-in-law in to see me and the baby even though I had not seen Diane. Terry arose from his rest a few hours later. When he tried to call friends and family about Diane, they already knew what she looked like. Terry was crushed. The next day he came to my room to tell me he had just set up the high chair. I laughed to myself. The poor guy was just trying to be part of this big day.

What was the urgency that they should see the baby before me and Terry? Why did my mother have to be there at ten in the morning. Remember she didn't drive and Joyce had two small kids? *Click...*

I drove home from the hospital, so Terry could hold the baby. I didn't care; I wasn't very maternal. Diane was absolutely gorgeous; she had such a perfectly shaped head due to her rear end birth. We lived in a small apartment, which my mother walked to everyday to help me. God knew I needed all the help I could get.

Diane was about two weeks old when Carol brought her mother to see her. Carol and I played with Diane, bathing her over and over, changing her clothes, and combing and re-combing her hair.

Finally, Mrs. Parker said, "Take me home, you two are still little girls, playing with a doll, that's a real baby,"

I guess I wasn't prepared for motherhood, that's probably why God made her so good. She was very well behaved and even when she was an infant and I would tell her "Now is not the time to cry", she would stop and start smiling.

Diane was a beautiful little girl. I dressed her in pretty frilly clothes and she has always been cognizant of her good looks. When she entered kindergarten, I was sure she would be the next Eleanor Roosevelt (Even though I'm a Republican). At the end of that school year she got her report card. Her first grade teacher was to be Mrs. Weinert. She was my first grade teacher, and I went across the hall to her to announce this repeat of history. I was told "Young lady, if you expect me to remember all of the students that I have taught in my many years of teaching, you are sadly mistaken." I immediately turned around and said, "Look at the back of my head. You had me stand in the rear of the room facing the closet. Now do you remember me?" She failed to see the humor, turned and walked away.

Diane was then transferred to Old Mill Road School. Brian was about to start kindergarten and that was our new bus route.

When my beautiful daughter was in the fifth grade, I was teaching religion at Sacred Heart Church, and I had many of her classmates in my group. It was her eleventh birthday and she wore her pretty, pink Easter dress. Some of her friends told me how she was crying in school because she was made fun of for wearing a dress. My mother-in-law who bought the dress was furious and wanted me to go up to the teacher and complain. Instead, I went out and bought her carpenter overalls .She still looked beautiful and was very happy. Clothes matter so much in Merrick, even in elementary and junior high. When money was tight for us we managed to get her Jordache Jeans so she would fit in.

High school was another struggle for "D". We didn't know about her learning disabilities until her freshman year and that was a big hurdle to overcome at such a late time in her education. But she did it. We were very well known at the Bellmore Merrick Central High School District. At one point they didn't give my daughter an oral, unlimited time Regents. They said it was her responsibility to remind the school that she was LD (Learning Disabled).

Now let me ask you what sixteen year old kid is going to say, "I've got learning problems. You have to teach me differently."

Are they crazy just thinking she would do this? Well, it got to the impasse that either we were suing for discrimination against a learning disabled child or they would throw out the Regents and give her a passing classroom grade towards graduation. She got her credit because we were going all the way to the top. A cousin told us to contact the Nassau County Bar Association. They promptly gave us the name of the child advocate attorney, Steve Scharoff, who was working for Diane and who later became our personal lawyer.

After a short tumultuous marriage in 1987. Diane set her benchmark very high. It was difficult to believe that she would be able to achieve her ambition, but she did.

Diane is now a paramedic for the Police Department. She has struggled to achieve all she has. Her awards and commendations are many. She has preformed procedures most doctors and trauma centers would have been fearful to do. As a result, there are many children in pre-school rather than a cemetery.

Terry and I are very proud of her compensating for her dyslexia, passing her state boards, and being named "AEMT of the Year" by the county. Despite our having to eat roast beef, mashed potatoes, and string beans for dinner after dinner, we go to every affair where she is honored.

Brian

We moved into our home in September of 1966. Within a month I was pregnant with Brian. Born on the first of July, he was the largest of all of my children, tipping the scales at eight pounds at 3:54 am. We often refer to his hour of birth as LAST CALL. He has worked in numerous drinking establishments as a bartender, and that is the time you can order your last drink, before the bar must close.

Brian's birth wasn't tough; he just was a challenge from there on .Brian never walked, he just started to run and he hasn't stopped yet. Even as a toddler, he had difficult habits. For instance, he liked the sound of crashing glass, so he would take silverware out of the kitchen drawer and throw it up the lampshades just to hear the light bulbs break.

Diane and Brian shared a room. One morning, I'm not sure how, but she got hold of a package of 101 needles. She threw them all into her brother's crib. I thought I had removed all of them, but one needle had imbedded itself in the mattress. I had put my baby down for a nap. While he was sleeping, that one missed needle came out and went directly into Brian's eye. The head of the needle went straight in and touched the back of the eye and then came straight out. It makes me cringe to think of it. When I picked him up after a short two hour rest, his eye was a little red. It was then I realized for my hand brushed up against the lone needle. We called Dr. Stola, our GP, but he said to take him to an eye specialist, we went to a Dr. Bedrossian immediately, then to a radiologist. Dr. Zwanger. While we were waiting to have the x-rays taken, the technician asked if I was pregnant?

I replied, "Yes"

Boy, did I get a weird look. As if to say, you can't even take care of these two kids and you're having a third. In fact, she was kind of right. Motherhood was not my strong point; it's amazing that all four survived without permanent damage. Poison control knew my voice. When I called, they would just say, "Which one? Drank what now?" Maybe I was calling about Diane drinking antifreeze or TJ gulping turpentine; thankfully, he had herpes in his mouth that made him spit out the stinging liquid.

Brian started school in Old Mill Road School with three other little boys from Gianelli Ave. His teacher was pregnant and only worked to Halloween, then the district brought in a teacher named Roberta Lachs. I volunteered to work on the kindergarten Thanksgiving feast. I thought the new teacher was fine. In January, the bus driver told me the teacher was leaving; I was appalled that children with their first school experience were about to have their third teacher before half of the term had expired. I went up to Old Mill with a fire lit under me. I couldn't believe the unprofessional way this situation was being handled. Ms.Lachs refused to speak to me; she claimed I was one of the parents who was forcing her to resign. I didn't know what the hell she was talking about. I finally found out that there was three families who had mistaken information and met with the principal, and the board was accepting her resignation rather than look into the false allegations. Well, along with my neighbor and friend Judy Haberstroh, we got a petition signed by forty-four other parents and half of the faculty. Our petition was to have the board refuse her resignation and have her stay. We presented our petition with a group of several dozen people, including lawyers and the local newspaper <u>Merrick Life</u>.

You probably know what happened, Roberta and I became friends. She remained with the North Merrick School District # 29 until she retired some twenty odd years later.

Brian's next teacher was a delightful woman named Mrs. Block, She was also Diane's first grade teacher. As Brian was entering second grade, we were delighted with his teacher, Annette Montanile. She had a reputation for being very strict and getting the most from her students. Just what we were looking for. As the old saying goes, be careful what you wish for …you might get it! Well we did. On open school night, we experienced a sterile classroom, a hospital would have been more stimulating to learning. Of course none of Brian's work was displayed. Came spring, Brian came home from school with a three inch gash in his face.

I asked him "What happened?"
and he said,
"I fell in the bushes"

I wanted to know if he saw the nurse. He told me it happened at the end of the day, right before he got on the bus.

Later that evening he confessed to lying and told us that the filing cabinet had fallen over on him when both drawers were opened simultaneously.

We asked, "Why didn't you tell us the truth earlier"

Brian said, "I don't want you to be mad at my teacher because, she will hate me more."

The next morning I was up at that school in a heart beat. By the time I got to speak to Ms.Montanile, my fury had grown out of proportion. This teacher told me how much she loved all of her students. Bullshit! I told her that I teach four year olds and they are a lot cuter, but some just turn me off. The trick is you can never let the student know that you don't like them .And, if they feel you don't like them, then you are wrong because the feelings of the child can't be wrong. Because feelings are never right or wrong.

She wanted to know who did Brian's laundry. He came to school in the morning with clean clothes, but, when he came in from the playground, he was a mess from his rough housing play.

I said, "I have four children, but I send Brian's laundry out. Who do you think does his wash?" My sarcastic mouth was at it again.

His teacher then proceeded to tell me that Brian was back one hundred and fifty spelling words.

My response was, "When were you going to inform me?"

She said, "I sent you notes."

Upon inspection of Brian's crammed desk, there were the notes. Never delivered. I wanted to know why she didn't call or contact me through Diane or TJ's teacher. No response.

Now I wanted to know if Brian was being promoted. She said, "Of course."

Now I wanted to know why my son, who was so ill-prepared could possibly be ready for the third grade?

Within moments, I was in the principal's office. (because of my involvement with my children's school, I was friendly with her). She suggested that Brian be transferred into one of the other classes and I agreed.

That afternoon, while Brian was playing with his other friends from the block, I heard him say;

"I did it. I got out of *Monstermmeal's* class"

I opened the window and yelled out "You little son of a bitch. You're not getting out that easy."

Back up to see the principal again. Now Brian was going to bring his daily work to her and she was going to monitor him until June. Brian went on to the third grade with Mrs. Lannick, a great teacher.

Brian was always the class clown. As a teacher, I know what a pain in the ass that type of student is. But Brian is still extremely witty. Brian is truly one of the funniest people I know.

Brian is a very physical person, his large body is extremely strong, and he's a bull. Sometimes bull-headed.

Brian has been on the New York City Fire Patrol for over fifteen years. This group is employed by the Board of Fire Underwriter's Insurance companies. Their job is to protect what has not been damaged during a commercial fire. He also works for the NYC Fire Department Union and has since 9/11.

Brian is one of the most generous and forgiving people alive.

The Toys

We were hard up for money, we didn't handle our bills responsibly. We were in our house a little over a year and not managing two babies, a mortgage, the utilities and trying to keep up with the Fire Department's social schedule.

"God forbid" we were to miss one of their spectacular dances or parties where the conversation was interrupted (compliments of a Fire call) in mid-sentence and resumed with the rest of the sentence three months later. You sat at the same table with the same people and discussed boorish topics. Thinking back I seem to remember them wearing the same outfits. (Some, I believe are still wearing them now, forty years later). Any similarity to intelligent conversation was purely unintentional. Finally, after many years of mundane searching for notable signs of intellect within the confines of this organization, we made friends for life with John and Kathy Puglisi and Dick and Gail Kmitis. But, I'll get back to the Fire Department later.

Back to the neighborhood, Adele Oakley was the first person I met on the block. The stories she told me about my neighbors were absurd, but I later found out they were all true. Adele never missed a thing. It would be obvious that she and I would become friends. Because we were friendly, we would gossip all the time.

One day in the fall of 1967, right after I gave birth to Brian, she told me that she was invited to a toy party. This really peaked my interest since Tupperware was becoming so overdone and boring, plus I was looking for a way to bring in much-needed cash... A few days later I saw an ad for Mutual Home Toys in Massachusetts. We went to see Marge Hoffman, their representative in East Meadow. Marge was a pleasant woman, not a pushy salesperson, who lived in a brick Cape Cod house in a middle class neighborhood, She had a small room in her house set up with the entire toy line. I figured, if this woman can give up a whole room, this could be a lucrative endeavor, I signed up immediately! I thought this was my panacea and it proved to be. My first hostess was Maryann Garrett, the party was $88.00. I found my calling. I like to talk, and, for a few hours, every eye and ear was on me. I was the center of attention, I liked this position, my demonstrations were taking more time and I was developing my own comedy routine and perfecting it six nights a week. And I was making good money. The following year I switched to American Home Toys, also in Massachusetts. Their local representative was Bernadette O'Connor. This company had higher benchmarks for kit repayments and for bonus requirements. I was taking a huge risk, hoping to earn $35.00 to $50.00 a night. A few years after I went to work for American Home Toys, Mutual went out of business.

After four years, I became an area supervisor. I was thrilled with the new position and the double commissions I made. To be a supervisor, you had to have at least five people working under you by the end of September. Amy was born the first week of August.. When the Regional Supervisor asked me how many girls I had, I replied two girls and two boys. (Speaking of my family). Boy, was it embarrassing to find out she was speaking about business and I was talking about my children.

One year, Terry was on strike over the Christmas holidays. The strike started right after Thanksgiving and lasted fifty-nine days, and, because he was paid Railroad Retirement instead of social security, we didn't get any benefits for a long time. Thank God for the toy money. It was the only thing that got us through; we had the toys from the kit for our children's gifts and the money for our substance. When I had more than one kit, I would donate the second set to the Knights of Columbus that Terry belonged to .The toys were valued at $500.00, and it provided a pleasant holiday to those less fortunate and a needed tax write-off for us.

Our Regional Supervisor was a crook; none of us realized she was fudging the books. She blamed the company for all the problems we were having. As a result, all of the Long Island Region decided to break away and start our own company; we were all mortgaging our homes to start the new business. The president of the company was coming to New York City for the annual toy show; he called and invited many of us to join him for dinner. I responded that I would not attend, that I was leaving with EEEEEE and making the new company, All my new partners and I were told about the embezzlement. EEEEEE was fired, and, luckily for her, had no criminal charges placed against her. We were asked to pick our own new Regional Coordinators, and we did, and continued for many more years.

Bernadette O'Connor and I worked together for a few more years until she moved back to Ireland. Before she left, however, she invited Terry and me to a mysterious meeting. We went out of curiosity, only to find out about a new movement in the Catholic Church, Marriage Encounter.

We committed to make a Marriage Encounter in March of 1973. ME teaches a system of communication between a husband and wife. It can be so emotional that it can either make or break a relationship. When we came back from our weekend, we had no one to share it as the O'Conners were already back in Ireland. I called Mary Ann and Ray Garrett to try to get them to try Marriage Encounter, only to find out that they had made one the month before we did. Then I asked why didn't they call us.

They said they were getting so many people mad at them because they wouldn't stop talking about it, and that they didn't want us to get pissed too.

One day while I was at the toy warehouse in Deer Park, I was told to beware of a swindle that was permeating the toy companies. It seemed that a large shipment of racing car sets were stolen from a New Jersey pier. The thieves were trying to push the merchandise through toy parties. The lawbreakers were responding to the ads that were placed for prospective demonstrators. Ironically, I received a call that very evening; I played along and set up a meeting to get the stolen goods. I immediately called the police and a contact was made to apprehend the culprits. My brother Philip was there, furious that I got myself involved. He felt that law enforcement was not my job.

The contact was set up for the local A&P; I was supposedly shopping, while the man I was in contact with would be waiting by my car. When I came out of the store, I was shaking like a leaf, and armed with Clorox. I thought if he attacked me, I could have hit him with bleach and then throw it all over him. I can't believe I behaved like such an idiot. The individual approached me and the police apprehended him. Later, I found out he had a wife and two kids and was trying to make a fast buck the wrong way. The race car company rewarded me with a trip for two to the Downingtown Inn in Pennsylvania. I was a sleuth for one day and that was enough. My disguise for the next supervisors' meeting was a trench coat and dark glasses.

I became an annual speaker at the Boston meetings and made friends from all over the country. At each convention, I would room with people from outside of the Long Island region. To this day when I'm at a workshop or convention, I don't stay with people I can communicate with daily. I was always taught Network,

Network, and Network. Because of my choice of room-mates, many times I would come home with a southern drawl or a mid-western twang. My family was wondering what exactly happened in Bean Town.

The trips gave me my first plane ride and second and third. I was always winning bonuses and trips. We went to Bermuda, Hawaii, I won a cruise, but I had a broken leg and couldn't go. The company paid me the trip's worth and we bought a brand new truck!.

One company meeting, my roommate, was xxxxxxx, who was a grandmother, from the mid-west, who had to show proof at the bar, because she didn't even look eighteen We were working very hard and to relax on the second night we went to the hotel club and xxxxxx picked up a young guy, then took him back to our room. I ended up walking in on a very intimate moment. I left quickly, and was met by a Senior Superintendent, Buddy. He offered me a bed in his room which would have been very innocent, but the Bible Thumpers from Texas would have surely caught me. American Home Toys owner, Joe Diccio, the strict, Bostonian Italian Catholic, would never have understood. I was able to make a phone call to my Regional Coordinators, Fran Spinelli and Jo Cerevella and had to sneak into their room to sleep for the rest of the trip. The bible thumpers did catch me on the phone, but I told them I was calling my roommate, who had inadvertently locked me out.

I have always had stomach problems and generally have vanilla ice cream around to soothe me. When I stayed the night with Jo and Fran, I had to have room service bring me some. They didn't bargain for the guest and the Breyers melting in the bathroom sink. Only all this made for a very interesting convention.

When we were told that Joe Diccio was closing his doors, that was the first time I was ever top demonstrator in the state. Oh well...Now the whole Long Island region went shopping for a new company. We decided to go to a company called Toy Chest in Detroit. Well, again I became the top demonstrator in the state. Guess what? Toy Chest went out of business. Then most of us went on to The Price Party Plan in New Jersey and out they go while I'm the number one salesperson in New York.

Terry suggested I leave the home party business, as I was driving down the economy and hurting the industry...

Amazingly, enough, I worked at the toy parties for twenty-three years.

TJ

When TJ was born, we couldn't have been in worst financial shape. Handling Diane and Brian was a full time job and Terry wasn't making much overtime on the railroad.

When I was pregnant with TJ, we went to visit friends in Forest Hills, Queens; well they served marzipan, a very sweet thick pastry. I didn't make it home. Terry had to throw out the floor mats, to our new car, on the Long Island Expressway. Our whole family used the same doctors, many of us at the same time. My cousin Carol, Uncle Robbie's daughter, was pregnant with her son Damien and, my sister-in-law Carol was expecting daughter, Jill in August. I didn't start going to the gynecologist until February. TJ was due the end of April, I was putting off the doctor's payments as long as I could. Even though I put off my doctor's visits as long as possible, I made them all up in one day.

On the day my son was born, I went to the doctor's at his Merrick office at nine am. They told me to go home. At eleven am, I was given the same advice, but not to eat. Ha-ha, we went straight to McDonald's. The two o' clock and four o' clock visits told me I could go to the hospital or wait it out at home. Obviously, I chose to wait it out and go to the doctor's, Levittown office at nine pm. During my day-long labor pains, I was talking to my sister-in-law Carol and discussing my dilemma, She had a scheduled appointment for that evening.

When I could hardly walk at seven pm, I arrived at the Bluegrass Lane office of my OB-GYN. Carol spotted me struggling up the sidewalk and started screaming,

"You bitch"

"You promised me you would wait `til after my visit"

My doctor said to Terry,

"How fast can you get to Hempstead General?" (The Hospital)

Well, Carol waited hours, for the one doctor left seeing patients. The other one left to be with me and my son.

TJ was born at 8:06 pm. Clearly it was a fast delivery.

When I came home from the hospital a few days after TJ was born, Carol Schutta, who was taking care of Diane and Brian, brought them home to me. While we were sitting and enjoying a quick cup of coffee, suddenly Diane appeared with five day old TJ.

She asked,

"Is this my new baby brother?"

I didn't show my panic for fear she would drop him on my cement floor. I gently removed him, but, I knew that I was not prepared to be the mother of three.

When I was planning a small baptism for my baby, my father was upset that I didn't ask all of his brothers to come.

I said, "Daddy, I can't feed all of your family"

He answered with his familiar response "Don't worry about it; I'll take care of it." And he did.

He went out and bought a ton of food and called up all my uncles and invited them. It didn't matter what I said or how I felt

When TJ was just a couple of weeks old, I came down with the mumps. It was the most excruciating pain I have ever withstood. The childbirth that I had been through three times paled in comparison to the agony I was suffering with a childhood disease. *Click...*

Terrence James McCauley Junior was a very bright baby. He was walking by nine months, and talking fluently by eighteen months. He was very independent and headstrong. He was the smartest in school and my biggest achiever.

We were at a Fire Department ballgame at a local school; TJ just turned three. He slipped on the playground slide and came crying that he hurt his arm. Like the great mother, I was, I kissed his boo-boo and sent him back to play. A little while later he returned, and I rubbed his arm until it was better. Again he was crying, so I gave him his bottle and his arm started to shake when he raised it. We took him to the hospital to check his fall further. The doctor who examined him said it was just bruised, but it couldn't be broken because of TJ's mobility. They x-rayed him just to be sure. Guess what? My little boy ended up in a half body cast for six weeks. Terry's remark to the doctor was, "You forgot to tell him what he could or couldn't do with a broken arm." What a summer that was. He still ruled the roost, he told everyone what do. At three years of age, he was arguing like a Philadelphia lawyer.

In kindergarten, he had Mrs. Lachs and would put her through the wringer to prove his points. All of his teachers admired his determination and drive.

He joined the school band when he was in the fourth grade. We went to Florida that spring and he got a terrible case of sun-poisoning. Even with large blisters all over his body, he managed to hoist his drum on his shoulders and march in the Memorial Day Parade.

He met Karen Slattery through one of his jobs. Karen was and still is a very attractive young woman. TJ's proposal to his wife was a magical moment; it was at the EAB Building's Christmas Tree. My daughters Diane and Amy were hiding in the shrubs and they managed to get every word and bent knee gesture on tape.

Their wedding was even more unprecedented, an elaborate bridal party with each attendant more beautiful than the next. The place: Sacred Heart Church, where TJ received all of his other sacraments. He and Karen were wed by an old friend of the family, Deacon Dan. Baldwin's Coral House made for a magnificent setting for a fantastic reception.

Karen's family, now our extended family, are truly genuine people. Sadly, my daughter-in-law's father died a few months after the wedding. "Slats" as he was affectionately called was very much like Terry. Joyce, her sister, looks a lot like Karen. Yet their personalities are as different as night and day. Peggy, her Mom, has the most beautiful grandchildren you could ever imagine. Of course I'm prejudiced because they are also my grandchildren!

My first grandchild was born on May 27, 2001; six months after, my world fell apart. If it weren't for his pending arrival, I would have committed suicide long before. I was able to get into therapy. I'm still alive, but the doctors and the drugs did help in many other ways.

I believe suicide is the choice of the individual; I don't think any one has the right to put a tremendous guilt on a determined person. Life should be a personal choice and death should be the same. If abortion is legal and that is the taking of another's life, than why is suicide condemned when someone is taking his/her own life? I truly respected and admired Dr. Kevorkian; he allowed people to fulfill their own destiny.

Karen gave birth to a beautiful baby girl the day before TJ's thirty-fifth birthday. Their daughter, we believed, was conceived on the 15th of August, a day of great significance to me. Kylie Mairead with her shock of dark hair and dark eyes is a welcome addition to our family. T.J. and Karen moved their little family to a very large home in North Bellmore when she was just seven weeks old.

Amy

Our youngest child, the most open and most poignant of our family.

Different right from the beginning! I switched to Dr. Davoli, a Rockville Center obstetrician, for most OBs were not into the new births. I wanted to have my fourth child naturally. Terry and I went to Lamaze classes, in a private house in East Rockaway. Our families were appalled that we were going through with this. Men didn't belong in delivery rooms. The hospital wasn't too keen on the whole procedure. I had to switch from Hempstead General to South Nassau. One delivery room nurse suggested that after I give birth I should throw my baby on my back and go out and work in the rice fields. The nurse wasn't that far out. The day I came home from the hospital with my baby girl, I had a toy party. Yes, so I packed my car with my seven boxes and off I went to work.

Amy had it tough; the others didn't welcome another in the brood easily. She was always very independent. My mother-in-law called her bossy Bridgette. I called her monkey feet. Why? Because, when she was in the playpen, she would take off her shoes and socks, and with here bare feet climb up the mesh and escape on her hands and knees. She couldn't walk, yet she could crawl like a guerilla sniper in a Central American civil war.

Her brothers and sister would always tease her and tell her she was adopted. She was a tow-headed blond and they were all brunettes. They would hide her toys and glue her pillow to the sheets. They would try to boss her around, but I always told her she didn't have to listen to anyone but me.

Nursery school was a harrowing experience for her and her teachers. Because she was so independent, she didn't listen to anyone but me. She was only three and she would terrify her playmates and infuriate her teachers. Amy was not going through life as the baby. She rose to a leadership role in the family, and immediately became a take-charge kid.

Kindergarten was another trip.

In the spring before she was to enter school there was a letter sent to thirteen parents in our neighborhood that stated that fourteen kindergarteners were being placed in a school at the furthest north building to our homes. The letter invited the thirteen families to an orientation at the new school. Of course I went to this meeting. The district principal asked me why was I at this meeting? My reply was "I can do the math and I know that my daughter, Amy is the fourteenth child." He responded that his letter would be going out in the morning mail.

To which I said,

"I'm here tonight, deal with it." There was no way we could stop the move of half of a kindergarten class, but I did get the superintendent to sign an agreement that when these youngsters entered first grade, they could go back to one of the other two schools of choice. So Amy had to go to North School for kindergarten, the school I was at for four years. During her term at North, The Superintendent suffered a heart attack and died, so the agreement had to be honored by the new super. Not a good start but we had a very healthy rapport for the next six years. While I had the good relationship with Dr. June Irvin, Amy wasn't having it in the class. Once, at recess, she was on the see-saw with Kim Greaves, the little girl who lived across the street. Well, it seems Kim got off the ride while Amy was still in the air. When Amy came down, she went after Kim with a vengeance. The teacher interrupted, but no way was she going to stop Amy. When Amy was trying to kick Kim, the teacher told Amy to relieve her anger by stamping her foot into the ground. She had to be kidding–that wasn't going to work with my little maverick. She told the teacher, "You can't tell me what to do, only my mother can tell me what to do." When the teacher tried to physically show Amy how to control herself, Amy kicked the teacher. Amy was suspended in kindergarten for three days. We didn't care. We were pulling her out to go to Disney World. anyway.

We went to Florida in our trusty 1966 Ford station wagon with our cabin tent packed on top. The trip down south was agonizing and Amy did nothing but complain. While we were in the wonderland of the magic kingdom, she would never let us see her smile. If she saw us looking at her, she would start scowling and say,

" I want to go home, I want to go to my real home, not that tent" We should have shown more compassion for our little five year old . She was never treated like a baby, but she was and is still ours. When we were on our last day in the park, Terry and I were trying to figure out how many coupons we would have to purchase to get into the haunted house . Well, Amy started her whining and crying for the thousandth time, Terry finally just hauled off and belted her.

Two old ladies exclaimed,

"Oh my God, did you see what that man did to that little girl?'

With that, Terry picked up Amy by her shoulders, and carried her over to the women and said

"Here lady, you take her, and, if you don't hit her, you're a saint."

The look of shock on the faces of these stunned seniors, as Terry walked away was staggering. I had to go retrieve my hysterical five year old. All the way back north, she was relentless. There was no consoling her— finally Terry threatened to throw her out of the car.

At one point, in the middle the night, Terry pulled off I-95 and told Amy to get out! When she cried,

"Daddy don't make me get out, I don't know where I am." Terry replied,

"You're in South Carolina, now get out"

She promised she would be good and for the next 800 miles all we heard was "Daddy. Am I being good?"

And who would have believed that we returned four years later? She was much better on that trip.

Eight days before Christmas, while Amy was still in kindergarten, she had the flu and was vomiting blood. Terry was working when I took her to our new family doctor. Dr. Metz, a very good doctor with a thick German accent. He told me Amy had to be admitted to the hospital. She didn't understand him, but she caught on when his nurse offered her some plastic jewelry to wear in Lydia Hall Hospital in Freeport. Then the fight ensued, she wasn't going anywhere without her daddy. Terry was working, but he knew when he left that this might have been a possibility. He knew I was taking her to the doctor and why. Well she fought all the way there and then when she was admitted, she kept yanking out every IV they put in her arm.

I finally convinced Amy to let me go home and get Terry who was due home within the hour. I didn't let anyone know about Amy until I could tell her father. It was snowing quite heavily and it took us longer than anticipated to return. But when we did get back to the hospital, the chill was colder in the pediatric ward than out side on the front steps. We knew immediately something was wrong. The security guard told us we had to speak to the charge nurse. UT~OH "What the hell happened?" We only left her for an hour and a half. What could she have done? My sweet little innocent daughter, had decided she wasn't staying there. She got herself completely dressed, had gotten to the far end of the hospital, past every guard and sat down on the steps at 9:30 at night. When asked by the security guard at the door, she said she was waiting for her grandpa to come pick her up, that he drives a black and white taxi cab. Every cab driver in Freeport knew who my father was and she would have been found by her Pop-Pop. I would have been dead. Fortunately, the hospital got her back inside before she escaped. When we got there, they removed her clothes and shoes and coat and locked them in a nurse's station closet.

I had to call my parents and tell them she was in the hospital. What if she escaped again? When I called, my mother answered. I asked for my father. My mother's response was "Who is this?" *Click...*

To punish the hospital, Amy went on a hunger strike while stealing the Christmas goodies patients were bringing in for the staff. No wonder we couldn't get the results from the hospital's tests. She was a tyrant, she beat up a little kid who just had surgery on his nose; she wouldn't let her 13 year old roommate use the bathroom or the TV. After a week, my mother asked what would happen if Amy missed Christmas? It was like setting off a time bomb. Once again we had a screaming kid on our hands. Christmas was going to be the day she came home. She didn't have a calendar and would only listen to me, *Remember* "You can't tell me what to do, only my mother can tell me what to do." Well, on Christmas Eve, they determined that Amy must have ruptured a blood vessel in her esophagus and the blood was appearing when she was constantly irritating it. She was fine. They called for us to come and get her within seconds of Dr. Metz's signing of the release. They were so happy to see her go that they handed us, her confiscated clothes and told us to leave. No one said, "Goodbye."

Amy met Michelle Menfi before she started school. Michelle's mom was Brian's den mother. All through grammar school they were close friends. In junior high the friendship continued and each would do anything for the other. Well, I was working at Twin Oaks Nursery School and Day Camp and I received a call from Ben Ciuofo the principal of Brookside Junior High School. They said that Amy was an accessory to attempted murder. I almost laughed out loud into the phone when I realized this was not a prank. I went straight to the school. It seems that Michelle had a fight with another girl and brought a carving knife to school just to intimidate her. When word got out that Michelle had this weapon she slipped it to Amy in the lunchroom, promising never to reveal where the hidden knife was. Not three minutes later, the school authorities came looking for Amy, and so much for never giving her up. The worse part of the whole situation was that Terry was on his way to the principal's office. The school figured that was a worse punishment that they could ever impose. They are still fast friends, Amy is the godmother of Amanda, Michelle's teenage daughter.

Amy went to the prom with J.J., a great looking guy with this rat type pony tail. Terry told him to lose the hair, but of course he didn't. He was a loser and eventually ran off to join the carnival in Minnesota. I swear this is true. And I'm not making any of this up. Carol was a mutual friend of Amy and JJ . . . She followed him out there. She met someone, married him, and had a child.

Amy received her Associate degree in two years and is currently working on her bachelors. Her major is accounting; she is a clone of Terry's mother in every way. Her physique is definitely that of her grand-mother's. She, like her Nanny, is a very capable and diligent employee, a take-charge bookkeeper that companies relied on constantly.

At the end of May in 2004, Amy called her father. She was deathly ill. When Terry got to Northgate Electric in Melville, LI, where Amy worked for eleven years, he found her on the floor writhing in pain. The assholes she worked with just stepped around her. Terry and his brother rushed her to the hospital; she was admitted to intensive care with pancreatitis, a life-threatening condition we had never heard of. It occurs when gallstones block certain digestive ducts and start to infect and poison the body. After weeks in the hospital, her *humane?* job ignored her. They didn't believe she was sick, When she returned six weeks later, they fired her for a bad attitude. This was one of the best things that ever happened to my daughter, though at the time she was devastated. She now works for a company that appreciates her for the wonderful person she is, the person who goes the extra mile for someone else.

Aunt Dolly

A unt Dolly is something of an enigma. My mother's younger sister is eleven years her junior, but you would have thought them to be twins, sharing the same DNA.

When we were growing up, Aunt Dolly always spoke her mind. My father and she had a cordial relationship, but not a loving one. In fact I believe it was more of a love-hate connection. Aunt Dolly is my godmother and is still very near and dear to me.

Since the death of my mother, she is my second mother. When I was growing up, it was Aunt Dolly who bought the special outfit for my sweet sixteen. I remember the light cranberry sweater and straight skirt set. I wore it until the skirt was too tight and the sweater had more pills than a drug store. If I look deep in the eaves of my house, I might even find it again. When Terry and I got married, my aunt bought us a dinette set-brown Formica, the Danish Modern style of the sixties. I still have the bottom piece of the server twenty five years later. But the gifts are not what I remember the most, it was the attention she gave me.

After my grandmother died, my mother's family came to Merrick to see us a lot. They all lived in Brooklyn and we lived in "Lonng Eyelind". I really don't remember too much of the Alvino side before that.

My grandfather lived with Aunt Dolly and Uncle Billy. Grandpa was a shoemaker when he first came to this country. I vaguely remember my grandmother. I guess I was about three or four when she died. She was carrying laundry up the stairs when she fell, she didn't survive the accident.

When I was in my early teens, we would go to Brooklyn so my mother could see her father.

We had a car with a rumble seat, it's a seat built into the trunk. When you are sitting in it, you are on the outside of the car. With the wind whistling through your hair, it seemed like it would be fun and adventurous. In all actuality it scared the shit out of me. But I always wanted to go back there, despite the fact my brothers were threatening to throw me out on the Belt Parkway. I couldn't cry and get to my mother to tell. I would just have to crawl down into the back of the car, behind the rear seat. I was just too scared to move.

Grandpa couldn't speak. He had his larynx removed years before (Throat Cancer) He would hold the portable microphone up to his throat and he could communicate with us all. When we got to grandpa's, he would coax Philip and me into his room to give us some of his homemade licorice juice. My mother would start yelling, "Don't you give that to the kids"

He didn't listen to her. She was only our mother after all. He was our grandfather, and he could give us his special drink, anisette.

To this day, I still love the liquor.

Aunt Dolly married my Uncle Billy and they had Carol and Vinny, and, of course, grandpa.

Nursery Career

Terry had overslept several times and had what the Railroad called a miss. Because he had three within a year, he was penalized and furloughed for thirty days. The layoff came in February. While we knew when it was going to take place, at that time, there still was no toy money coming in because the season was over. I had to get a job while Terry stayed home with Amy and TJ, ages three and four.

The newspaper had a position for a nursery school assistant teacher with mini-bus driving. I told Terry I was going to apply, but I didn't want to do the driving. When I interviewed with Lily Monty at Playmore Nursery School in Freeport, she told me she already had someone who was reluctant to drive. At which point, I started with my bullshit of how I love to drive and I feel it's part of the child's school day. I started immediately. I hated the job, it was so boring. You couldn't talk to your co-workers, you just had to keep your eyes on the little ones. I couldn't wait for it to be over, but I promised I would stay until June. Terry had to go back to work. I couldn't say anything. Finally, I told Lily I was leaving– she had already suspected as much. She said, "How many reasons do you have that are pre-schoolers?"

I answered," Two"

She reminded me of the commitment I made to her and that I would have to bring my reasons to work with me. When I said I couldn't afford the tuition,

she said,

"I wasn't asking for money"

So I started my teaching career and my two youngest children received a wonderful pre-school education, Now it wasn't so bad that the teachers weren't allowed to socialize, now that my two babies were in the school. I learned to appreciate it and love it.

That summer Lily told me to stay home and to bring all four of my kids to the small camp she ran.

You don't find many people with that type of caring and generosity. I'll never forget Miss Lily Monty.

Two years later Lily sold the Playmore Building and closed the school. I went to work down the block at Twin Oaks. The Hoffmans and the Ellmans had bought that day camp and school just a few years before. It was a school twice the size of Playmore, now it is ten fold larger. Three of my kids, Diane, Brian and Amy, worked at the camp for several summers. The friends I made go back twenty five years and are near and dear to me. The summer before TJ and Karen got married, I returned to Twin Oaks as a driver and cartooning counselor. Four year old Little Terrence will be a camper at Twin Oaks.

Meanwhile, Terry and I were very much involved in Marriage Encounter, a religious communications method used to help strengthen marriages. Believe me!

It works! We wanted to push our involvement even more, so we went on a "couples" retreat, Antioch. This was held in another parish and then we brought it back to Sacred Heart for the high school youth. It was called a Christian Awakening. Every week we would have about six or seven kids discussing vital issues for them. The popularity of our group grew and grew. By that summer we were up to forty or fifty students. We held the get-together outside and we worked with a seminarian, now pastor of Holy Redeemer Church in Freeport, Father Rich Figliozzi. The group eventually was spilt into different parishes, and went into their churches for weekly meetings.

First Throat Operation

The toy parties were taking their toll on my voice. I talk a lot to begin with and then to talk non-stop for two hours night after night was the straw that broke the camel's back. I was very hoarse. It sounded like I was running a zoo. It was getting worse and worse, and, when the toy season was over, my voice did not return. Never being big on going to the doctor for anything, finally I had no choice and no voice. I had polyps on the vocal cords; my family referred to them as friction burns. Whatever you call them, they had to be removed. It was May and I had to arrange everything for my children. I made the hospital arrangements for after Brian's First Holy communion and after T.J.'s birthday and my mother's trip to Florida.

When I asked my mother to help me by babysitting for T.J. and Amy for three afternoons while I was in the hospital. My mother said she would get back to me. I didn't hear from her for two and a half years. I didn't hear from my brothers in all that time I wasn't asked to any family functions; my kids were ignored at midget football games. Their birthdays were non-existent.

Terry had a job handling things. He was not Mr. Mom. The night before the operation my frazzled husband called me at the hospital and told me to cancel everything, that I had to come home immediately. The kids were driving him crazy, he had them for four hours. Yeah, right I just hung up and wouldn't answer the phone again. Then I made arrangements with neighbors and marriage encounter friends to watch the kids while Terry was at work.

During the time of my unexplained banishment, my father would stop by to see me and my kids without my mother's knowledge.

My Aunt Sophie questioned my mother why she didn't help me. Neither she nor I got an answer.

Eighteen months later, I had to be operated on again., This time the condition was worse than the first. Again, friends and neighbors babysat.

My mother contacted me when my father went into the hospital ten months before he died. I drove her back and forth for visiting hours. The babysitting never came up.

Bermuda

American Home Toys was my place in the sun. I loved to talk and still do. I love to be in the limelight and in control. The toy parties afforded me all of these opportunities and paid me nicely. I had risen to the top supervisor in my region. I had a few supervisors working directly below me. As a result of my successes, I won several trips. One was to Bermuda.

The trip was scheduled for April of 1977. I was thrilled about winning the trip, however, I needed to retrieve my birth certificate from Suffolk County, N.Y. My mother gave me a souvenir birth certificate from a hospital out east, but I was unable to get the proof of birth. They told me there was a mix-up. When I asked my parents, they both said in unison that I should use my Board of Elections Card to prove my citizenship. *Click…* I thought this very odd because if my mother said "White" my father would always say "Black". This was the kind of relationship they always had. When I followed their suggestion, I didn't have any problem going on my trip but I often wondered how my parents knew this simple solution as they were not worldly people. *Click…*

I went to see Philip; I wanted to know what's up. I said jokingly, "Am I adopted?" *Click…*

Phil answered, "Yeah, and whoever left you on the door step was there two years earlier with the same basket that dropped me off." He said, "Look in a mirror, we have the same face." It reminded me of the time my niece, Jill was born .Jill is Philip's youngest daughter. When she was in the hospital, her mother called me and said Jill had a terrible nose. It was her father's nose, but Carol, Phil's wife lamented. No girl should have to go through life with this nose. When I responded that Jill had the same nose that I had and it didn't cause me any problem in life, Carol didn't know what to say. The conversation changed quickly.

The trip to Bermuda was wonderful, We really had a ball. Tom and John were the other supervisors from New York to win the trip. The guys were gay, yet Terry and I were comfortable with them; nevertheless, most of the people on the trip weren't. Before departing the four of us met in the lounge at JFK Airport. While we were having cocktails, the guys told us that they had a superior grade of marijuana and they invited us to smoke it with them in Bermuda. Tom and John had been to the tiny country several times and had numerous friends. In fact, they were bringing a can of white paint to one of them. The flight was flawless. When we arrived in Hamilton, Bermuda a bus for American Home Toy personnel was on hand to take us to the hotel. Well, Terry, Tom and I made it through customs, but John was stopped. We knew he had the grass on him and we were preparing to be expelled from the country for transporting drugs. Customs were sifting the paint, but John had concealed the MJ in his shirt pocket and we finally were able to go to the hotel. On the cab ride there the guys were singing, "I want to be in America, Everything free in America." Terry and I knew we were in for a great trip in more ways than one.

While in the guy's room, I tried the marijuana for the first time. I said, "It had no effect on me at all." But an hour later, when we rented motor scooters, I hit a bridge of coral and was on the ground cackling like a hyena.

Terry said mockingly, "No, that didn't effect you at all."

On the plane Terry and I wore LI is for Lovers "T" shirts. Joe Dicicco was a little leery of Tom and John, but his kids were enthralled with them .They were the spark of Bermuda, they had personal friends and knew so many people. We had all the clubs and night spots greeting us. Diane and Joey, the boss's kids, came out with our foursome. On Saturday night Joe and his wife Anna had asked us to kind of keep an eye on the situation. We left the group at four am, we just couldn't keep up. And the next thing I remember is my boss telling me that his son had the waste paper basket next to his bed and had missed mass.

My Father Marries, Dies

I n the fall of 1976, My father was fixing a tire on his cab when the jack fell on his left foot. Daddy had diabetes and the extremities are very vulnerable to this terrible disease. He went into Nassau County Medical Center, formerly know as Meadowbrook Hospital, now known as Nassau University Medical Center. They tried medication to clear the gangrene that was setting into his small toes. It didn't help. Finally he had to have a few toes removed, then he had another toe then the other two. The doctors said the infection had gone too far when they took off his left foot and eventually the leg right below the knee. In March of 1977, he was fitted for prosthesis and walked out of the hospital on April 1, 1977, April Fool's Day. He immediately went back to driving his cab; they needed the money desperately.

My father had developed bed sores on his right leg because of his four month stay in the hospital. He was in excruciating pain and in May he couldn't continue to work. It was Ascension Thursday, a Catholic Holy Day forty days after Easter. My father called me to the house. He said he needed a priest and I should call one immediately, I said, "Daddy, it's a holiday. I can't get a priest today."

He said, "You know everybody at the church, you can get me a priest." Well, I called my friend, Father Dan Harren, and he agreed to come.

Two hours later he arrived on his motorcycle. I thought my father was going to have a stroke when he heard the big hog pull into the driveway He accused me of bringing him a phony priest. After five minutes, they were fast friends. After an hour and a half, I found myself arranging a wedding.

My father's hospital records provided his blood test, I took my mother to the clinic for hers and then we were off to the bureau to get the license. Of course I couldn't resist the opportunity to tell every body in the town hall that it was for us and that we were lovers. It made my mother laugh, and we were legally set up.

It took about another week for the Diocese to finalize the papers. On Monday, May 24, 1977, my mother called me at Playmor, and told me Father Harren would be there late in the afternoon. I left work immediately and went home I called my parent's brothers and sisters and told them about the wedding. I called my brothers and told them they were going to be the best men. I was the Matron of Honor. They thought I was nuts. Then I went to the only bakery opened on a Monday and got a quarter of a sheet cake already decorated for a wedding. Somebody never picked it up the day before. I went to Park Ave. Florist and asked for a bridal bouquet and I waited while they arranged it. The neighbors thought something happened to my father until they saw that the way I was dressed and the cake I was carrying was a sign of celebration.

All ten grandchildren were playing in the backyard when Father Dan's motorcycle pulled up.

My nephew Joey started yelling, "Come on, everybody. We have to go in. Grandma and grandpa are getting married."

My father was mortified . He said,

"Get those kids in here and make them be quiet." Ha! I guess it was his pain medication that was making him delusional.

After the ceremony, we had champagne in plastic glasses and I made a toast and told Father Harren, "Now if anyone calls me a bastard, I can punch them in the nose." My father was embarrassed again. *Click...*

After the family left, my father asked me to take him to the hospital; he needed to have his right leg amputated. I didn't want to be mean but I said, "No, not on my mother's wedding day. I promise I'll take you first thing in the morning." At 6 am, I took my father to the hospital; he was operated on days later. My brother, Ceasar, worked diligently on getting my father's cab in pristine condition. We wanted my father fit for a second prosthesis; he was very reluctant. We were going to have the cab fitted with hand controls, but Dad refused to even talk about it. We brought the cab to the hospital for him to see; he wouldn't go near the window. He made up his mind that he was never going to drive again, and he didn't.

My Broken Limbs

T.J's cub pack was going on a roller skating trip to Levittown Roller Rink; I had to ask my neighbor, Linda, to watch Brian and Diane, while I took Amy and her brother to the outing.

Linda made a remark, "Don't break your leg."

I think she put a hex on me. While I was going around the rink with Amy in tow she kept slipping and sliding. Instead of letting her fall, I foolishly kept trying to help her balance on her skates *Wrong Move!* I should have just let her fall. I didn't instead she just tumbled. That's what happens to seven year olds but not when you're thirty three.

When I heard the cracking sounds, I knew I was in trouble. I asked Carol Ann Braun, a former sorority sister whose son Kenny was in the same pack as T.J. to watch my little ones, and get them away from all the fuss. I gave them a $50.00 bill to buy refreshments. I wasn't in pain – I was just delirious. I didn't want to alarm my two small kids. Carol went to watch my money and my children. I went to the hospital.

Carol brought Amy and T.J. home, but I didn't get home for four more days. I had broken my tibia and fibula. I was in a cast up to my hip for five and a half months.

My mother was visibly upset. I was in the same ward as my father when he died just a few months before. The sight of the cast bothered her because when they amputated my father's leg, they placed a cast-like bandage to the stump.

Terry was very sweet. As a surprise he washed and waxed all the tiles in my house.

P.S. We had no carpeting at all.

When I arrived home on the fifth day, he was very upset that I was getting plaster everywhere.

My response " What kind of an idiot, washes and waxes every surface I'm trying to move on. Do you want me to break my other leg.?"

Guess what? Five years to the day I broke the other leg.

The big bulky cast never held me back. We did everything. When our trusted station wagon died a respectable death after giving us a decade of service, we were left only with our Volkswagen Bug. We were waiting for a brand new Chevy Suburban (that we had ordered the previous January) that didn't come until the end of summer.

We went to the beach, to summer concerts, to block parties. I even struggled through volleyball games.

We went everywhere in the little "Herbie." Terry removed the passenger seat, I sat in the back with Amy and Diane next to me, Brian was on the floor in the front holding the cast on his lap. T.J. was on the little ledge behind the rear seat, the shelf inside the car over the engine compartment. Obviously, this was before the day and age of seat belts. And for the McCauleys we were satisfied though completely unsafe, but too oblivious to notice.

One morning, as the kids got ready for school, they were mismatched in old scruffy clothes. I said something to Terry. He said he had no laundry to do. He told them, if they needed clean clothes, they better bring down their dirty laundry. That night, when he opened the wash room door the clothes fell over him. It took him days to catch up, but, at least, they didn't go to school looking like abandoned children.

Depression

In 1981, I suffered a deep depression. That was when I was first diagnosed as a Manic Depressive. *Click...*

In my teenage years I always appeared to be jovial and happy. I strove to be the class clown and was disappointed that I wasn't voted most humorous or at least most talented in my school yearbook. However, I demonstrated, strong suicidal tendencies and would leave notes but my mother would find them hidden in a lamp base or under knick-knacks. When my mother confronted me with these notes, I didn't respond to her because of my fear of being labeled "sick in the head". *Click...*

I was always hyperactive, but I never realized how I fluctuated from one extreme to another. Of course I never associated these high school instances as part of my disease. The stomach problems that I constantly had, I attributed to my peptic ulcer. And I accepted this physical answer to my discomfort and anxiety. *Click...*

About this time, the psychological stress put a great strain on my marriage and I was having great difficulty dealing with my family. With Christmas approaching I was more and more depressed, but I did not recognize the problem. In January of the new year I asked my husband to move out. I never told my mother or brothers about this, the only one who knew was Carol. The following month during the mid-winter recess, I cleaned my house and straightened any miscellaneous paper work that was left undone. Since I was never a great housekeeper, this was a monumental chore. On Valentine's Day (Sunday) I wrote a long letter to my children, who were with their father. I tried to explaining my decisions. And then I took every prescription and non-prescription drug in the medicine closet. *Click...* I didn't expect the stomach medication to stop the peristaltic action in my stomach and therefore it slowed the effect of the drugs entering my blood stream .A couple of friends, John and Kathy Puglisi, stopped in to see me after going to 5 0'clock mass. They immediately called the Fire Department, John was the chief and he transported me to Nassau County Medical Center for a drug overdose. While I was in the emergency room, a nurse passed a nasty remark about how the attempt was not successful. This caused me to get irate and to try again in the hospital, but the only thing I could get my hands on was the vials used for extracting blood for tests. This time I drank the liquid in the bottom of the tubes. *"Click"...* Keeping silent about my latest deed, I was then transported to a psychiatric unit at Mercy Hospital. Naturally my blood tests were now very erratic. No one ever knew about the vials and what I did until this writing.

John told Terry what was happening and he packed up the four kids and brought them to his mother's house. She was told not to contact my family and she didn't. She didn't think that mental illness was a serious disease; she thought it was a cop-out. My mother and brothers did not know I was hospitalized nor about my separation. I hid the facts or my whereabouts from all I could. *Click...* While at the hospital,(I was treated for 22 days), I found it was very difficult to accept the psychiatrist's diagnosis of Manic Depression. After all I was the jokester and the life of all the parties. I had to **Have** control, that was what this was all about. For the first 10 days of my incarceration (and that's what I felt about the hospitalization), it was excruciatingly painful. I was under a constant suicide watch; someone named Donna would sit at the foot of my bed all night. In the morning I would get up and growl at her and ask how much they paid "Watch Dogs" in this hospital. I was pissed because I received no response from the *German Shepard* (Donna). I refused any phone calls or visitors. I refused to take any medication; I refused to take the Maalox prescribed for my stomach. I was paranoid, *Click...* I thought they were trying to chemically get me to justify the reasons why I was there. *Click...* After five days, my hospital assigned psychiatrist told me he was not accepting any "more shit" from me and that if I didn't start taking the prescribed drugs voluntarily, that I was going to be admitted to a lock-down ward. *Click...*

Another patient had given my name to my pastor, Father Harold Langley, who literally snuck into the hospital pretending to visit the informant. He was such a great man; he and my faith have always helped me through those terrible episodes. He died of a heart attack in the early nineties. What a loss to all who knew him. I found out a few months after my release from the hospital that Terry was also seeking consolation with him. *Click...*

I was smoking about three packs of cigarettes a day. I always said, "If you want to become an instant millionaire, just have a cigarette concession in a psych ward." The depression worsened with each passing day until a nurse called my brother, Philip. He told my mother, and Ceasar and my family were there that night. A few days before my family was called, I had a terrible argument with Terry in the hospital. I was allowed to go out for four hours on a Sunday, but I refused to see any one, including my children, the powers that be would have allowed me to meet with them in Mercy's lobby. I declined.

Fortunately, my friend Maryann Garrett never got the message about my reclusive behavior. She just walked into my room and God knows, she was sent there that day. I needed to talk to someone that day– I just didn't know it. After intense therapy and lithium, I was scheduled to have Electro shock .The threat of this procedure was a horrifying thought. Gradually, I began to respond and was doing better, but my new friend, Kathy, who was in the same room with me, was discharged. My depression took a big step backward. Again, I was doubled up on drug and contact therapy. Finally, I was forced to leave the hospital after 22 days. By this point, I didn't want to leave the safety of the hospital even though Doctor Freud would agree that I needed more hospitalization. My other doctors (Blue and Shield) insisted upon my leaving. In time my medication was changed to Ascendant and I visited my doctor twice a week, eventually group therapy replaced these solo visits.

Terry and I were still separated and I had no place of solace. My mother stayed with me, but I kept leaving the house and just driving around. Every time I would pull over and park so I could cry or think, people would just look out their windows or come out of their houses. I would have to leave; nobody welcomes a strange car parked by his / her home. Most of the time, I would go to Jones Beach. No one bothered me there. But there were a lot of others there with me and I wasn't sure why those cars were there either. But the summer that followed found me even more depressed, if that was possible. Not only was I entertaining suicidal thoughts, I now was contemplating how I could bring my children with me. I needed help quickly. I quit working the summer camp immediately and contacted Mercy Hospital, the very same day. These were very terrifying and scary times. I needed to return to solo visits, as well as out-patient group therapy for an additional nine months. Over the years I realized I was a classic case and that I followed the perfect script of Manic Depression, Bipolar Disorder in every detail. Now my only hope, when things get really bad, is myself. This is a disease where you are constantly fighting to get control of yourself. The fight never ceases and the highs of mania hopefully get longer and longer and come more often. However, when it goes the other way , you strive desperately to reverse. But, you are on an uphill battle all the way. My best recourse is to retreat. One time I disappeared at a cousin's who was sworn to secrecy. I let my family know I was alive and that I would be home in a week. I just had to remove myself from the situations that caused me all the anxiety. *Click...*

The Questions

When I came home from the hospital, my mother stayed with me. I was so fragile and I was so overwhelmed with my own life. The medication, I was taking, Ascendent, made me behave like a zombie. I was numb to mostly all that went on around me. My mother came to try to cope with my kids who felt abandoned and I couldn't deal with them or her.

Terry and I were still separated and he now had other interests. Whenever he came to the house, it was horrible. I couldn't deal with him. I was vicious and wouldn't give an inch.

My mother was kind to Terry, but I wouldn't budge. I was making him pay through the nose. I even changed the phone message to "This is Ginny McCauley, I'm not available to answer the phone right now. If you are looking for Terry McCauley, You can call him at his Mommy's # xxx-xxxx" I knew when he called, it would piss him off. It did, and I didn't give a damn.

On one of the days he came to pick up the kids and he said something about the message. My response was to spit in his face. Needless to say, things were getting progressively worse. My mother tried to say something to Terry, and he said to her that she didn't even know who I was.

She was very hurt and upset with his remarks and all she kept asking was, "What did he mean by that?"

I just assumed he was referring to the problems that we had going to Bermuda. That was the only thing I could come up with for his statement. But I don't think my mother bought that reasoning. *Click...*

Another Depression

In early July of 1986, another serious depression I couldn't handle, was in full swing. I knew I had to retreat. I packed my clothes and told Terry I was going out. I started to drive around not having any idea of where I was going. I started to drive out east and thought I could find my cousin, Deanna's. When I got to Blue Point, I figured I could find her beauty salon. Instead I saw her car pulling away from her shop and I followed her home. I scared the wits out of her. She realized she was being followed, but didn't know who it was until we got to her house. I stayed with her a week, sleeping in my aunt and uncle's part of the house. They were at their home down south. I asked her not to tell anyone I was there and she didn't. I let Terry know I was alive and well. He had called my mother in Florida thinking I was there. He never let on that I wasn't home. I don't think my mother ever knew. I came home at the end of the week. I was able to cope much better. I didn't know the real bummers were coming in the next few weeks.

On July 29th, my Aunt Dolly called from Florida to say that she took my mother for a checkup and the doctor immediately put her in the hospital. He told her she had lung cancer. My mom was a very heavy chain smoker. She had been hospitalized before for emphysema; she spent weeks in intensive care. She beat it then. She would this time too.

The Trial

Terry was in his second year as Chief of the North Merrick Fire Department. The NMFD was scheduled to go to training in Bethpage. Terry called a drill to get the men to go to the Fire School. One of the Fire Commissioners, who lived a few houses from Terry when he was growing up, hated him and his brother. Charlie Kerns is one of the most evil men you could ever meet. He never wanted Terry to be Chief and he was going to do anything and everything he could to destroy Terry's fire-fighting career.

Charlie charged Terry with calling in a false alarm and brought him up on departmental charges. If this wasn't bad enough, *Someone?* called the newspapers and now we were hounded by reporters.

Most people thought Terry would take this and cowardly accept their punishment. However, our lawyer read the charges in the paper and called us from upstate to say he would be there for us.

My mother was still in the hospital in Florida. I needed to go to her, but she insisted that I stay in New York to help my husband.

A kangaroo court was held at the fire hall on Wednesday, August 6, 1986. When Steve Scharoff, our attorney, walked in, the court reporter told one of the commissioners that they better beware. Steve was great, but the bias in that fire hall was so flagrant, and Charlie Kerns refused to remove himself from this fiasco, despite the out and out testimony that he had a pre-planned vendetta against Terry and his family.

Even one of the commissioners had admitted that they heard Charlie Kerns make a threat that he would get Terry no matter what

For hours, as our neighbors listened, and finally got the chance to speak at what was supposedly a public hearing. Over one hundred came out in support of Terry and spoke about the travesty of justice. It all fell on deaf ears because the Fire Commissioners who bring the charges, then proclaim themselves as the judges and jury. Naturally, they found Terry guilty. The Supreme court supported Terry four months later. He returned to the fire department but his heart was not in it. By the way, the unfair practices that the commissioners used have now been changed. The kangaroo court is now presided over by an impartial hearing officer, appointed by the county. As for me, I always hated the place and my position has never changed in all these years.

I said it before and I'll state it again, "We will go to all lengths to prove the point." I kept pushing and Terry was very anxious to be vindicated.

The next morning, on August 7th, Terry and I left for Florida with Diane.

Florida

The three of us drove for two days before we reached New Port Richey. This was before the days of cell phones so we weren't sure of what we were going to find when we reached Florida

My brother, Philip, along with my niece Judy, had been at my Aunt Dolly's house since the first of August. When I got to the house at 10 pm on Friday night, I went to my mother's room only to find out that Philip had taken her home from the hospital the day before but had to admit her to a nursing home that day. Philip had spoken to Ceasar, but there was no way to reach me. On Saturday morning, Philip and Judy left, Terry, Diane and I went to the home.

My mother seemed comfortable, for the next two days I was going to the visiting hours and making fun of my mother's comatose roommate and everything else around her just to make her laugh and to try to help her forget her pain..

On Monday, one of the nurses asked me "Who is Ceasar?"

I said, "He's my oldest brother. Why?"

She said, "Your mother is waiting for him before she dies."

My response was "Fine, let her wait ten or fifteen years."

Then she told me that I didn't have those kinds of options.

I still couldn't believe my mother wasn't going to beat this, as she had done twice before.

Ceasar arrived early Tuesday morning. Terry and I picked him up at The St. Petersburg's Airport. He flew in from Newark. He didn't depart from Jersey until two hours after his arrival time. The wonderful People's Airline had taken eight hours to get my brother to Florida.

When we all got to the nursing home, my mother insisted on me leaving the room. *Click...*

After Ceasar spent sometime with my mother, we all decided that he should drive back to New York with Terry and leave me with my mother and my aunt.

All of a sudden the nursing home wanted to know the name of the undertaker that I was going to use in Florida. I was horrified. I couldn't believe them. They told me that they weren't there for my mother to get better, but just there until she died. My mother and my aunt's friend knew of a funeral parlor. I was appalled by the fact that I was making arrangement for a living woman, whom I loved and still didn't believe was going to die.

On Friday, at 1am, Philip called to say my mother died. It was August 15, 1986, the Feast of the Assumption.

The "assholes" at the nursing home called him instead of me. After all, Philip was twelve hundred miles away. I was one.

I immediately called the home to find out what had happened? They responded by telling me to call the Funeral Home.

To which I responded by saying "Who the fuck do you people think gave you the name of the funeral parlor?"

All day Friday, my relatives from Florida on my father's side came to pay their respects. On Saturday, Aunt Dolly and I brought my mother's body back to New York, along with one measly suitcase with my mother's things.

Losing my mother was far worse than I expected. First of al, I never accepted the fact she was going to die. Secondly the lack of compassion was compiled by the "notifying" confusion. The home said that my mother would possibly rally before she died. I was minutes away, I stayed in Florida, so if something happened, I could be right there with my mother. But it just didn't happen that way and I was cheated of the final moments of her life.

The plane ride back to New York was quite somber but the worst of the nightmare didn't begin yet. Aunt Dolly stayed at Philip's during the wake and funeral. I needed my alone time.

Late Saturday night, I was on the phone with Carol. I needed to vent and I always turn to her. During our conversation, Katy, our large Old English sheepdog, was going wild. I couldn't calm her down. Finally, I let her out, and, after a few minutes, she quieted and I let her back in the house.

Sunday afternoon was the first session at Walker's Funeral Parlor. When Terry and I went to get into the car, we found that three of our tires had been slashed. I then knew why the dog was so upset.

Can you imagine the rage we felt ?I couldn't even get to my own mother's wake .We called the police, they intimated that somehow my own family was responsible. I recounted that "They were waiting for my mother and me to return to New York. I was sitting in coach and that my mother was in cargo in a box." Later Terry said I was cruel to the cop. I said, "Fuck the cops."

Of course it was never discovered who vandalized the car. But I'll bet they have a Maltese cross on their jacket. And it was just coincidental that one of the firemen got married the day before? Jeez do you think someone was drunk? And people wonder why I hate this vindictive, malevolent organization?

My brothers called to find out why we weren't there? They came and got us. Their language was even worst then mine At least they understood my pain.

When the fire department hypocrites came to the wake, I asked them to leave and I refused their sympathy. I believe they had some hell of a nerve showing up at such a personal gathering for the purpose of mourning where they were considered the adversaries. It was my mother's funeral, and, if I wanted to be a bereaved bitch, I was going to be and no one was going to stop me or even try to.

Sacred Heart School

In June of 1986 Carol called and told me that there was an opening for an Art teacher at Sacred Heart School in Cambria Heights, Queens. I went in to meet Sister Margaret Igoe, (Peggy) a very sweet cordial Dominican nun who had been principal for two years.

In order for you to teach at any Catholic school you must have your own church contact the school to vouch for your commitment. I had told my Pastor, Hal Langley. He had written to the pastor of that Church, but because both churches have the same name, confusion resulted. Thus, I never knew that I secured the position until right before school had started.

Unfortunately, my mother had died two weeks before the first day, and my mom never knew I got the job. I know she would have been so proud to know I was not in nursery school anymore but with an elementary school. She would have considered it to be a step up in my professional career.

I found myself in a room that had all kinds of garbage and very few art supplies, but I ordered the basics and took on the kids. I enjoyed the friendship of a large faculty of twenty five.

I never forget the day, I had a sixth grade class and we were making collages. The kids were noisy and the room was a mess. All of a sudden some of the kids said, "Sister Margaret wants to talk to you."

I looked around the room. The door was closed, I didn't see her, so I just ignored them. Then I started to hear her calling my name, I still didn't see her.

Then she said, "Your room is too noisy" and requested that I should quiet the students down. I still didn't see her! One of the kids pointed toward the ceiling. Finally, after a few minutes, I realized she was calling me over the P.A. system. Duh!

I finally said, "Sister, YOU can hear me."

When she replied, "Yes Mrs. McCauley I have been listening to you for five minutes. It's too loud in that room. Please see me after your class."

The next thing I heard was "Oooh" from the class. Kids love when the teacher is being scolded.

My first year at Sacred Heart, I was there only three days a week. Tuesday and Thursday in the upper school, grades first through eighth. On Wednesdays, I worked for Sister Francis, Principal of the Nursery, Pre-K and Kindergarten program. These classes were held in the rectory basement.

I eventually went full time; I started to do fundraising. My experience with the toys really helped out.

Carol and I enjoyed being with each other all day but didn't get a chance to socialize. It was very different from the team teachers of three and four year olds. Terry couldn't understand how we could be on the phone for hours each night after we just spent the entire day with each other.

Carol's classroom was directly under mine. I had invented an ingenious way to communicate with her. I took a bell and tied it to a very long ribbon and dangled it out of my window. Whenever I wanted to talk to Carol, I would attach a note to the bell and ring it. Carol would answer by writing her note and ringing the bell for me to haul it up. Our own private AT&T. One day Carol was ringing. I immediately pulled up the message which read "Mrs. McCauley, can you tell me why this bell is hanging outside of the school?" The note was signed Sister Margaret and went on to say I should see her after class. I was in trouble again.

Faculty meetings were always my downfall. My mouth and humor weren't always welcomed. At one such meeting in 1992, we were asked to pray for Cardinal John O'Connor. Some one inquired about his being ill. To which I replied he had a heart attack when his daughter ripped up a picture of his boss on national television. I was only kidding when I was referring to the activist, Shinead O'Connor, tearing up a picture of the Pope John Paul II on *Saturday Night Live*. Carol laughed a little; I had to remain after the meeting.

At one monthly meeting, Hazel, a sixth grade teacher presented Carol with a puppy. The six week old didn't make a sound the whole meeting. Carol insisted I go home with her to tell Joe about the canine surprise. She said he wasn't going to believe her gift.

Joe wasn't in the house five seconds before the puppy found its bark. They had the dog for thirteen years.

On the sixth of February in 1991, I was in a car accident. Two cars crashed into each other and then both of them came sliding into me while I was at a stop sign I wasn't even moving. I was out of work for months. Since no one was there to do the fund-raising, my full time salary could no longer be met. I was being cut back to three days a week. I couldn't afford the cut in pay. I told Peggy that I would have to go to high school. Peg knew that meant five days a week. She didn't want to lose me. So she set me up with Sister Ave` Laffey, another Dominican, and now I worked at Saint Clement Pope in South Ozone Park for two days and was still at Sacred Heart for the other three.

St. Clement Pope

There was a world of difference between SCP and SH. Sacred Heart was the Mother Earth and Saint Clement was the Twilight Zone. Many a day I got in trouble for singing the familiar tune do do doo do (theme song). But I always get into trouble at school. I spent more time in the principal's office as a teacher than I did as a kid.

The students at SCP were not as disciplined as the Sacred Heart students. They were definitely more challenging, and much harder to manage.

Sister Ave` Laffey had quite a mystique compared to Peggy. In fact, their only similarities were that they were both Dominicans and very Irish.

When I went for my interview, Ave` and I got our directions screwed up. I got blamed, but I knew I wasn't wrong, so I accepted the blame and got the job.

The teachers were delighted to have me on board, I was about to be a prep period. A forty minutes break for them.

It was a needed job and everyone was great but it was an art teacher's worse nightmare **Art on a cart.** Four floors of classes, no elevator. I will say this two years of no classroom makes you very organized. I developed my own system and it worked very effectively.

From the first week in September, Ave taunted me about my Associate's Degree. Every one at SCP either had a Master's or was going to college for one. By the spring semester, I was enrolled in school.

Willie Mae was the pre-k teacher, a prim and proper black woman about my age. Willie was already attending York College, a CUNY school. York was originally a junior college and had become a senior college a few years before I enrolled. It was close to the job, but it was no NYU.

A composed Willie Mae never expected my registration to be so memorable. We went one day but they wouldn't accept a check or cash to register. I had to return the next day with a postal money order. I was extremely agitated; I guess you could say I was going POSTAL.

When my friend and I returned the next day, the line at the registrar's office was about twenty-six miles long. I wasn't about to spend hours there. I grabbed Willie by the arm and went straight to the front of the group. I reported to the clerk that I was there previously. She asked my name, To which I replied,

"Barbara Bush"

I loved Barbara for bringing the frump look back into the White House. I decided to impersonate her whenever an opportunity arose. I suppose I could have been arrested, but I still continued with my pranks.

Anyway back to my college registration.

When I told the not-so-bright desk clerk that I was Barbara Bush, she became so flustered that she started babbling to all the other employees that my name was "Barbara Bush." I think most of them were as dumb as she. The whole office was in a quandary; they didn't know what to do. I think Willie Mae was trying to hide, but I was having so much fun putting these people on. Meanwhile, the fuss was still continuing when the head of registrar came out of the administrative center and wanted to know what was happening. When he was informed who I was, he immediately took me into his office. He looked at my papers and said,

"Your name is not Barbara Bush!"

"Is she the first lady?" I asked.

His puzzled answer was, "Yes, but, your name is McCauley"

"And I'm the first lady on line? I guess that makes me Barbara Bush," I quickly retorted.

He signed the registration and said, "Welcome to York College, I think."

And so, I began my return to college twenty-six years after graduating from FIT.

Most of my art classes were from 2-6. Ave` let me rearrange my teaching schedule to get there on time.

Meanwhile, Sacred Heart wouldn't give me a minute of release. So much for Christian behavior.

Because I didn't have a full degree, my salary with the Diocese of Brooklyn was only 90% of a full degree teacher. I taught from 1986 to 1993 at Sacred Heart when Sister Peggy left for another position. Ms. Smith, a former colleague, became the new principal. A self-proclaimed *Christian* woman! Well, not to me. She decided that my pay should be cut by five thousand dollars a year. I found this out on the fifteenth of September, even though the *"Christian"* knew of the salary reduction since the middle of July. She waited until the school year was deep into the third week of the term to drop this on me. I asked her to call the Diocesan office to verify this predicament. The Diocese told her that she did not have to cut my salary– it was her choice. Well, the kind-hearted, yeah right, new principal refused. Several teachers tried to intercede on my behalf. But the *Christian* wouldn't hear it. She kept saying that if I continued to get my previous salary it would be as if I were receiving a bonus over everyone else. So I packed up that very day and drove to Saint Clement, where I switched to a five days a week for the next four years. I not only got my Bachelor's, but I also got my Master's while at SCP.

I was Dean of Discipline and with that job came four lunch duties a day. I had to agree it was the only way Ave` could justify a full time art teacher. I needed St. Clement's for my student teaching credits so we both benefitted.

My pranks still continued. One day when an aunt came to pick up her naughty, seven year old nephew.

Ave` said, "Take him out of here. He's nuts."

The aunt went ballistic that Ave` called him "nuts."

The next day I brought in a nice gift bag of mixed nuts. I forcibly convinced an eighth grader to bring the present to Ave`. The kid begged me not to involve her in my scheme but she never had a choice. Even the students were aware of my shenanigans.

The package had a sweet note attached that said,"Please accept these nuts, I will make sure my nephew behaves" The note was signed *Mrs. Filbert*.

A few hours later, when Ave said nothing about the strange gift and note, I went to her office where she promptly offered me some of her treasure. She then proceeded to read me the note. When she got to the signature, she realized my play on words and what I had done. Angrily, she said, "I'm going to **KILL YOU**."

Laughingly, I said, "What's the big deal? You're eating the nuts."

That's when she said, "I called the aunt and thanked her for the them."

"OH-OH"

The kid didn't return for the next term. But he was really "Nuts."

At the faculty Christmas party which I organized we decorated people as Christmas trees complete with lights and spray tinsel. That was fun but my choice of music had me under the gun again.

I'm Italian, so we sang *Dominic the Donkey* constantly. Again Ave` was pissed at me This time I didn't have a clue about what I did.

But she let me know that she was a SISTER OF SAINT DOMINIC and that many refer to the Irish as Donkeys, Wow! two strikes with one swing. I didn't even know I was up to bat!

Sister always had the money for parties. She used to give all of her staff $100 bonuses. She knew the neighborhood couldn't support the Christmas spirit– they were too poor. She was the best money manager the school ever had when illness forced her out. The school didn't last three years without her. In fact the school closed its doors for good in June of 2004.

Across the hall from my office was Alice Modica's first grade. Alice and I became soul mates. We weren't Ginny and Alice, we were Lucy and Ethel and many a time we didn't know who Lucy was and who Ethel was. I had someone who appreciated the pranks and would go along with them. We would call at the top of our lungs to each other by our staged names. Alice and I applied to the Board of Education for licenses in 1995. She was called for a position immediately, but she refused. As for me I was told my license might expire before I would get to use it.

York, Queens, and Far Rock

I truly lucked out by attending York College; it was less than two miles from SCP and four miles from Sacred Heart. When I had a two o'clock class, I could also take another class at six.

I was on the fast track and pulling away fast. One semester I had a 3.9 average and was carrying nineteen credits while working in three different schools with a student body of 750. Whew, I'm getting out of steam just thinking about it. I made a lot of friends at York and graduated "Magna cum laude." I only had one problem with an ass of a design teacher whom I unfortunately had three nights a week. That idiot stated at the class orientation that he never gives an A. That no one should complain about their GPA, because he doesn't care.

Well when I got all Bs and it spoiled my GPA I called him on the phone and told him to watch out, that Lorraina Bobbit was my cousin and taught me all I needed to know.

Languages were never my thing. I remember my high school Spanish teacher telling me after I wrote my homework on the blackboard, "Any similarity between this and Spanish was purely coincidental." I dropped the class, I was so humiliated.

But I had a lot of friends and I needed the language for my degree I had to cover ten chapters of conversion and translation. We formed a "Union"; each of us tackled one unit and copied the other nine. I didn't even do well on my one. But the professor and my fellow students got me through. Ole`

When Commencement Day arrived, I was the only white person out of 746 graduates. The Reverend Floyd Flake gave a very long-winded address that lasted 53 minutes. That day it was a bazillion degrees, with over a thousand people under a tent. When finally coming near the end of his speech, he stated that if he was in his church he would ask for an "Amen."

At that instant my daughter, Amy jumped up and shouted, "AMEN." End of speech.

Three years later when I started at Far Rockaway, a dear colleague and fellow alumna, Wendy Harris remembered the moment. It wasn't a monumental memory– it's just that my family were the only people not of color.

Through my undergraduate and graduate schools, I was still Barbara Bush. Now there were more first ladies, my neighbors.

We used to go to the movies practically every Friday. After the show we would end up at the diner. Our waiter was Tony and we were the First Ladies. I, of course, was Barbara Bush; Linda Greaves was Ladybird Johnson, only because she owned a parcel of land in Tennessee; Joanne Talbot was Nancy Reagan, complete with the red sweater; Pat Cassella was Pat Nixon; the first name was the same.

Our game with Tony went on for months. Sometimes, instead of the movies we would play miniature golf or go bowling. Once we went to a porn shop in town. Joanne and I went looking at the paraphernalia, while Linda was frozen at the door. We would be so silly that we would be wetting ourselves with laughter.

I got new dentures, and, when we started to diner hop again, I made a huge mistake and had a peanut butter sandwich. With my mouth stuck together, while gasping for breath, all I heard was the belly laughs of my dearest friends. Well there went the neighborhood.

Joanne and I took my big Suburban to La Guardia Airport to pick up Linda. The parking ticket blew out of the window into Flushing Bay. We only had a short time to get inside. So we rushed to meet the plane, we had our sign "LADY BIRD JOHNSON". The passengers disembarking from the plane kept turning and looking for the former first lady. It was hysterical; people were whispering that they didn't know they had such a celebrity riding with them. When Linda finally reached us, she just kept walking. She was giggling and walking all at once. Then, the argument erupted with the parking lot attendant. Linda had to go to the bathroom but figured she could wait until she got home. The exit worker wanted to charge me $16.00 for a 20 minute time slot. I explained that the ticket was in the middle of the water. He wouldn't hear of it. Now I was mad and I blocked the only exit from La Guardia Airport. I refused to move. Linda was PLEADING, and I wouldn't budge. Joanne knew we were going to jail when they threatened to call the cops. I still wouldn't budge. People were honking their horns; the parking company had to open the other exit booth. A supervisor was called and he told me to pay the money and he would refund me by mail. I still wouldn't budge. Linda's eyes were beginning to float. I still didn't move. Finally they agreed to have me mail them the money. I didn't even pay the two dollars. They never got the money. Linda was delivered with a sprained kidney, but it was worth it. Pride Goethe before the bathroom.

After York's attention-grabbing graduation, I took off a semester. Then, I applied to Queens College for my Master's Degree. Even though I was going to another CUNY school, the admission was very difficult. My high GPA enabled me to start in February 1995. I completed my thesis and got my advanced degree in three terms, graduating with honors in 1996. I stayed at Saint Clement Pope for one more year...

I had been interviewed at many Long Island schools, but I knew it was fruitless. No county school was going to hire me because of my age and experience. They wanted young teachers to start on bottom scales and I was not in that group. So, in the late fall of 1996, I was going through a catalogue of New York City High Schools. It was for the graduating eighth graders to select the high school best suited for them. Well, I went through the book for the same reasons; I couldn't remain with the Diocese of Brooklyn much longer. I loved the job, but Terry needed to retire and I couldn't kiss up the salary to God any longer. So out went twenty or so resumes to any high schools in Brooklyn or Queens that had Art Programs. Many schools acknowledged that they received the applications but no one had any openings.

During the first week of February in 1997, **at 6:30** in the morning, I received a surprising phone call "Good Morning, This is Far Rockaway High School. Are you available to substitute today?" I was still half asleep and told them "I was unable to help them." The next two mornings I again received the same call. It was quite apparent that the person on the other end had no time to talk, but I explained that I already had a teaching position but that I would be available during the spring break as the Catholic school had a different schedule than the public school. Ollie, I later found out, wrote this information down and promptly called me the first day of my spring break. She gave me directions on how to get to the school, and an hour and a half later I found myself in a Special Ed. class. At lunch someone asked if I knew Richard McAuley, the guidance counselor.

I replied, "He's my father."

Boy did I get weird looks. First of all, the man spells his name differently but pronounces it the same. Second, he's a lot younger that I am. The joke forged a great relationship, father-daughter or mother-son which is his version.

My second day in the building, they put me back in Sped. Ed (Slang for what they called these classes). They have a separate area of the building that they refer to as the Wing. The rooms I had to cover were on the second floor. The minute I walked in the students had me pegged as *fresh meat* and a brand new target. They were all over the place going in and out of the room. It was then and there that my new greeting evolved "Hello, My name is Mrs. McCauley and I don't give passes." They were on the phone which was on the wall by the windows. My reaction was to take the phone receiver and hang it out of the second story window. A short while later the Assistant Principal showed up at the classroom and wanted to know why the phone was dangling and was I aware of this fact. I informed her, I dropped the phone out, and, since I knew no one in this school, "Who would call me?" she promptly left. I worked as a sub at Far Rockaway High School for six days. After this, they offered me a position for the following September and I have been there ever since.

My first term, I taught nine classes of freshman art and one class of Living Experience, and, to this day, I'm still trying to figure out what the hell that was? My 3rd period class was also my last which was this nonsense class, which I basically made up as I went along. This group of youngsters was my substance and being at the "Rock". The affectionate name of Far Rockaway High School. We had an uncanny bond, we started high school together and fifteen of them stayed in the Arts until graduation in 2001.

When I started my second year, the school had approved of me teaching advanced drawing and so it began. Eventually, I was moved into a humongous classroom with thirty oak easels and a lot of very talented painters. The last page and the last line of the 2001 yearbook said, "My name is Mrs. McCauley and I'm giving you passes." I still see and hear from many of these and other graduates, several of whom are in college for Art Education.

Now times are rough at "The Rock" and I don't know how much more, I can take.

The bullshit is finally getting to me. As of September `05, you will find me teaching at Martin Van Buren High School in Queens Village, NY.

Alaska

had booked a cruise from Alaska to Vancouver. I was recovering from foot surgery. Terry was trapped in New York City for days; it was the Blizzard of 1996 that kept him hostage. Nevertheless, I was able to get travel agents to deliver brochures to my house. He was thrilled when he finally arrived home after four days in NYC to see pictures of ice covered mountains and fjords.

In April I started to contact the state. I was trying to get my birth certificate as I was traveling out of the country again, but this time Canada would no longer accept the Board of Elections card and I contacted New York State Vital Statistics in Albany. I was on the phone to Albany for three days. They were even calling me at work which at that time was Saint Clement Pope in South Ozone Park. On the last day of May while talking to a friend, Cheryl from Sacred Heart School, my previous school in Cambria Heights, I was telling her of my unsuccessful efforts and she was chastising me for breathing heavily and asking when I was going to quit my filthy, unhealthy habit of smoking. Cheryl was a physical Education teacher and was trying to educate me... My response was, "Tomorrow," so on June 1, 1996, I quit and haven't had a cigarette since.

Aunt Dolly called daily to find out how I was making out with New York State. I didn't understand how someone on a fixed income could afford to call me all the time. One time I remarked to my cousin Pattie, my mother's sister, Fae's daughter, that something was very odd. Pattie agreed and said if there was a secret shared by any of the Alvino family, they would go to the grave before revealing it. *Click...*

After a month, of trying to get my birth certificate, I was issued a Certificate of **No Record Birth Certificate**. This stated in essence this is legal because I am because I say I am. I was informed that I could use this certificate and my Baptismal certificate and obtain a Passport. Finally Terry and I enjoyed a beautiful cruise from Alaska to Vancouver. Carnival Cruise Line was the cheapest and I figured the scenery was the same no matter which ship you saw it from. We flew from New York to Salt Lake City and then on to Anchorage, the trip took nine hours .But we were pleasantly greeted by cousin Vinny, not Joe Pesci. Vinny was just assigned to Elmendorf Air Force base, where he had just been commissioned a Major. Vinny is the youngest of Aunt Dolly's two children. I hadn't seen my cousin in quite a few years and we only got to spend a few hours together. We then boarded a bus which drove us to Seward, Alaska where the ship was docked. Just what you wanted to do after all those hours of traveling was to take a three hour bus trip. We made friends quickly with our table mates, all of whom I convinced that I had won this cruise on the show "Wheel of Fortune". I told them I won the big prize at the end of the show for guessing the answer "Mount Rushmore". It was amazing how many people saw me win the prize.

I also realized how much the ship's crew vacuumed. I told you I'm not a domestic woman so I kept finding out where the machines were plugged in and I proceeded to unplug them. The noise was deafening to me.

Terry once bought me a bumper sticker that said, "My only Domestic Quality Is that I Live in a House." So true. We had or should I say I had so much fun putting people on. As I said before, "I am a jokester."

Every time we left the ship for an excursion we would sing "Happbly Happbly Blirthday" to the staff. It got to the point, that when we would try to reenter, we didn't have to be cleared – we would just have to sing.

Florida Surprise, Daytona

It was the Christmas of 1997, when I decided to give an extremely extraordinary gift .I had bought tickets for the Daytona 400 *NASCAR* Race The Pepsi 500 is held on July 4th weekend. It was to be the first race ever under lights at the Florida track. I also purchased ten days stay at *Fort Wilderness, Disneyland's Campground.* I was also paying for the airfare to and from Florida for my four children and my daughter-in -law. Needless, to say this was a very expensive surprise gift to my family.

Terry was very concerned that I had not done any of the Christmas shopping so he decided to take the chore on himself. Boy, did my kids have a great holiday he was buying camcorders, VCRs and TVs. I couldn't say a word. The kids were ecstatic Christmas morning. I was in financial shock, but was very happy to be there.

We had purchased a brand new 1998, 5th wheel, Jayco Trailer. Terry and I drove the rig to Florida, but Florida was **burning.** Half of the events at Disney were cancelled, the smoke was everywhere and the race was cancelled. So much for the thousands that was spend. The kids flew back ,Terry and I camped back. One stop was Jekyll Island in Georgia.They were dredging the water and I contracted a bug. After two days we left the isle and went to Fredericksburg, Virginia. I started to get extremely sick and I had a terrible circular rash on my leg. I thought I had Lyme Disease. When I finally got home and to the doctor, I ended up in Mercy Hospital for ten days. I had Cellulitis. Fortunately I was at the hospital. One more day and I wouldn't have been alive. I got out just in time for my niece, Jill's wedding.

Terry' Retirement Party

Terry was the butt of most of my jokes. When we were married a few weeks, he wanted me to wash his hair. I didn't want to. I convinced him that he had lice. The poor guy was scratching for hours.

One time when he pulled off the road to pee, I drove the car away leaving him standing on the Sagtikos Parkway, not far from the King's Park mental institution. Then, he started taking the keys out of the ignition, but when we were in the chief's car, I would just turn on the lights and sirens. Now he thinks twice before stopping on the roadway. Just like he won't leave me alone at a eatery for the fear of attraction. In a very posh Connecticut restaurant, I persuaded the waitress that he was blind, he caught on when she brought his dinner and instructed him that *his potatoes were at two 'o'clock and his meat was at six.* At a different bistro, I convinced the server that he was just released from prison; he figured that out when he had an unusual amount of bread and water to eat. At my nephew, Raymond's wedding I told the bridal party that we were *swingers*, people were running from us the whole night.

The poor man had a lot to deal with for thirty four years; he deserved a great celebration. The kids and I planned a surprise retirement party. We decided to have it at The Irish Coffee Pub in Islip. Terry would never expect anything, especially so far away. The deciet to get him there was my cousin Deanna's 50th birthday. She was no where near 50, but he didn't know that. I spoke to my Aunt Betty in Florida, she is "DD"'s mom; she and my Uncle Eddie would be up from the south by the middle of June. I sent her phony invitations for the 50th birthday party and she mailed them to my house. When Terry saw the invitations he wasn't wild about going to Islip, but he had never seen the pub and he didn't know how splendid the restaurant was. My daughter-in-law, Karen's bridal shower was held there. Terry was retiring July 1, 1999. The party was planned for Saturday June 19, 1999, Father's Day was the next day.

I went to get engraved invitations, the price was very steep. The kids thought it outrageous, they were right.

Amy found a little kid's invitation that said, "Come to my party."

The invites were adorable little trains. We could not have designed anything more appropriate. The balloons were orange, silver and blue, the colors of the LIRR, and were attached to little metal train lanterns with tea candles inside. Diane found them in Ikea. Every little detail was so coordinated that the party was bound to be successful. The summer before I had met this Block Operator, Dave, while we were camping at Nassau Beach. He worked with Terry and, through him I got several invitations to Terry's Railroad friends. One of them turned out to be Deanna's neighbor and corroborated the birthday party story. Just plain luck...

Two months before the party, I had made a retreat for Easter with my friend Pat. The theme of the week was reconciliation and forgiveness. Terry and his younger brother, Jimmy had not spoken for thirteen years. The argument involved ancient history through the fire department and should never have escalated to the scale it did. So much had happened in both brothers' worlds without each other:

T.J. was married.

Diane was divorced.

I had completed years of college, and had earned two more degrees.

Jimmy had gotten married and was the father of two boys.

I had decided to send Jimmy an invitation to the party. My feeling was if he came, great.

If not, I would tell Terry, "I didn't invite him." Well, Jimmy called Brian to see if the invitation was cleared by me.

Brian said, "It was my mother's idea."

The tension before Terry and I arrived was obvious. Everyone knew about the tumultuous past. But no one knew what the future would bring. No one knew how this surprise meeting was going to be. It could really blow up and make matters worse than before. Jimmy and his wife sat between the Puglisis and the Kmitis, I guess Jimmy felt that was the safest place to sit.

Terry was completely surprised, or shocked. I'm not sure he has recovered yet. He hardly spoke to Jimmy until the end of the night. When he did, it was with a great big bear hug. After a group sigh of relief, there wasn't a dry eye in the room. Whatever had transpired between them in the past was completely forgotten in an instant? One of the best things I ever did was to invite his brother to the party. One of the bravest things Jimmy ever did was to come to the party.

The next day was Father's Day. Terry met his nephews for the first time. Patrick, nine and Sean, seven were a fresh spark of life to the reunion. The six cousins were together for the first time in their lives; it was the most memorable Father's Day ever. We adore those boys and regret the time we never spend with them. When September came, Terry would pick them up after school and take care of them until their mother got home from work. He supervised homework, and brought them to Religion and baseball practice. Since Terry and Jimmy's parents were long passed away, we became like surrogate paternal grandparents. But Terry became the "Nanny".

Our grandson, Terrence adores Patrick and Sean and when they are around him they are so loving and caring like he's their little brother.

Jimmy was a Chief in the North Merrick Fire Department when this reuniting occurred. He and his wife had to go to several conventions and their sons stayed with us. One summer we took them for a week in the trailer, they seemed to enjoy it and we certainly did. It had been a long time since we had young kids camping with us.

The Death of Carol-May, 2000

Terry, Brian, T.J. and Amy had gone to Richmond, Virginia for a NASCAR race. They left on a Wednesday night and were to be there until Sunday morning. Driving home with the trailer can take between six and ten hours. Richmond is over four hundred miles and trailering can be an arduous task. This is a spring and fall ritual that started a dozen years ago. My nephew Raymond gets the tickets which are scarcer than hen's teeth and my family used to meet up with Ceasar's. They leave on Wednesday in the middle of the night so they can be there and relax for Thursday night's truck racing. Friday evening is a Busch Car racing. Busch cars are smaller than the NASCAR Cup cars that race on Saturday, the main event.

I heard from them when they arrived in Virginia and everything was going according to their plans...

On Friday night, when I came home from school, there was a message for me to call my Aunt Dolly. She wanted me to call her back as soon as possible. Her voice on the tape was very somber and I was immediately disturbed. When I called her back, she told me her daughter, Carol was dead.

Carol suffered a brain aneurism on Thursday morning, she died Friday afternoon. My godmother told me that Carol's husband, Assho-e was having her cremated as that was her wish and that it would only be a one hour ceremony. I told my aunt I would come to Florida. But she said, "There is no point in coming, because everything is happening so quickly."

I tried to reach my family, but they were already at the races. Thank God for Diane. She stopped over for a while; she was working and she said that I should make the trip down to Florida. She kept saying over and over that I belonged with my family down south, and that if I didn't go, I would be regretting it forever.

My daughter was right. I booked the flight and called my aunt.

Her response: "You're coming to Florida for one hour?

To which I said, "I was hoping I could stay a little longer."

We needed a little levity at this point.

My cousin, Vinny, yes the same one we met in Alaska picked me up at the Tampa Airport with the A-hole's family. Do you get the idea that no one liked Paul, Carol's third husband?

I arrived in New Port Richey on Saturday morning. I slept at my aunt's, Paul's mother and cousin stayed at Carol's house.

My Aunt Betty and Uncle Eddie had a house in Spring Hill about twenty miles from NPR. I felt that the more family I could get at the service, the more comforting it would be for my aunt.

Monday at the mortuary the funeral director asked about the eulogy. Vinny hadn't planned on it, so he asked me to help him write something. A good teacher always has paper and pencil on her and *I'M a good teacher*. In my opinion anyway.

We wrote a suitable, thoughtful message which was a delicate chore. Carol led an interesting life that was uniquely challenging to her family. Need I say more.

When the appropriate time came, Vinny wanted me to read the tribute, which of course I agreed to. I was never one to back away from a podium.

When I removed the papers from my blazer's pocket, all any one heard was my aunt say:

"Oh my God, did she write a book?"

The muffled chuckles led the way for an interesting acknowledgement. I began with my cousin's name and her date of birth when my beloved aunt spoke again and said,"You have to talk louder! Most of us are deaf here."

More chuckles but not so muffled this time.

We left the funeral home and I took every one to lunch at Golden Coral, While there the dumb waitress asked Aunt Dolly, "Is this a birthday celebration?" Sometimes people don't use their heads before they run off at the mouth,

When we went back to the house, Vinny and I spent the next two days going through old photo albums. We found pictures of our mutual grandparents, aunts, uncles, and cousins. We did find one picture of me when I was eleven. I was with my brothers. The snap-

shot was taken in Fort Dix, NJ when Ceasar was graduating from boot camp. While Vinny and I spent an hour
going through all the old books, my aunt was getting
quite upset and was adamant when she kept insisting
we put the albums back. *Click...*

Trip to Italy

was teaching High School Advanced Art in my third and fourth year at Far Rockaway High School. I made a lot of friends; in fact, we had a special fifth period lunch period which was the envy of many who were not that fortunate to eat lunch with the special group. We used to have "Special Fifth Period Lunches" about once a month. I was very instrumental along with a few of my friends, in organizing the meals. You know I was always the pushy broad. We even had other lunch periods trying to share our monthly traditions. We became a very close group, both professionally and socially, so that when an announcement was posted for a trip to Italy, to be traveled during the winter recess of 2001. We wanted to join the tour. *Click*...

The summer of 2000, I placed a deposit on a trip to Italy. *Click*... The trip was very reasonable and I was going with a group of forty from Far Rockaway High School.

Terry and I had gone on an extended Mid-West camping trip. After six weeks out, we ended up in Monticello, NY at the summer home of my friends Arlene and Dennis Fievelson. I wanted Terry to meet Dennis so that when we went to Europe, he would be more comfortable. We chatted about insurance and they urged to get our papers in order ASAP.

The next day when we arrived home we immediately applied at the Freeport Post Office for our passports on August 30, 2000. *Click...* The passport application stated that we **had** to have the proper credentials to accompany the document.

Rejection Notice

On October 18, 2000, my 56th birthday, I received a letter from the Department of State / Passport Agency stating I was denied the passport. *Click...* Terry had received his passport the day before and I knew in my heart something was wrong. *Click...* The letter said that I had to furnish more documentation to prove my citizenship. It further stated that I had ninety days to obtain this information, and, if I didn't, I would never be able to even apply for another passport in my life. *Click...*

"What was wrong?"

And

"Why was all this happening?"

"Who could answer my questions?"

"Where would I go for help?"

I was just hit with another ton of bricks.

"Why?"

How could I not be a citizen? I was born in the United States, but yet my own government was denying me and treating me as an alien, but from where I don't know?

For the next three weeks I tried everything I could to get answers. I called Virginia, I thought Ceasar could clear up my questions; after all, he's almost nine years

older. But he was no help. Philip was no better. My
Aunt Dolly was even more vague and Uncle Pressy
couldn't think of any reason why I didn't get the
passport?

The Day Prior to Election Day

My oldest cousin, Victor died; his birthday was the same day as my Uncle Eddie's daughter Deanna.

D.D. as she was affectionately called lived right next door on Old Mill Road. My younger cousin and I were very close. She spent endless days with me and my kids. In fact, while she was a senior in Calhoun H.S, she was at my house so much that the school was going to charge me with contributing to the truancy of a minor. Terry had a fit, he told her to stop coming, but she didn't.

Deanna called to tell me about Victor's death and the funeral arrangements. As we hadn't spoken to each other in a while, we chatted about all the things that were happening.

I told my cousin that I had to withdraw my deposit on the trip to Italy. I expressed how disappointed and baffled I was. The last two weeks were so bewildering to me. I felt like a leaf that was blowing uncontrollably in the wind, a leaf that came off the only tree I was ever a part of and now I couldn't reach the ground.

I grumbled that every time I tried to go someplace, I always had trouble and I just couldn't take hold of it.

Listening to my gripes, Deanna just started to sprout information. First she said;

"Everyone knows, everyone knows."

I kept saying.

"What are you talking about?

"Everybody knows what?

What was DD talking about?

She just kept talking and talking and kept repeating that everyone knew.

"Come on, Ginny, you know what I mean."

I was so exasperated I said, "I don't know what you are talking about Just say it."

The next couple of sentences are burned into my heart. I just couldn't believe them.

Then in one breath she just blurted out, "Your mother is not your mother. Everyone knows your father had an affair and you were born and put in an orphanage, and grandma went and got you out and told Aunt Lily to raise you."

Infuriated doesn't describe how I felt.

I could hardly speak up, but I managed to say,

"How do you know this, Deanna?" I asked in frustration.

"My father told me when I was a kid," she claimed with an air of unswerving determination.

I was just a jumble of emotion. It was like being on the outer edge of a tornado. You are getting spun around and around, but you want to know what's going on at the core? I was scared of what I was hearing. I was afraid there might be some truth to it.

I had to get off the phone, but my cousin persisted, saying, "You're a mother. You know that there's a public record of every time a woman is pregnant and every time she gives birth."

WRONG, it's the child's birth that is recorded and processed with the Bureau of Vital Statistics. I know. I had been through all the red tape four years before.

When I finally hung up, I immediately called Philip. I told him what our cousin said, His response was: "You can't believe her. She's always telling tall tales; she makes up stories and has for years."

Thinking about what Phil had said, I knew he was right. I was still reeling, but I started to settle down. Of course, my next call was to Carol. A best friend was the anchor I needed. Carol grew up down the block from DD and she agreed with Phil. She remembered my cousin's wild fabrications.

That night was a restless night's sleep. Something in the pit of my stomach was eating at me. It was as if a rat wouldn't stop gnawing at foul smelling, rotting cheese.

Election Day 2000

The next day, I was so upset; I became more and more preoccupied with my dilemma. I couldn't focus on anything. All I could think of was myself and my predicament. Instead of having questions answered, I was faced with more questions.

Plus the fact, I was pissed. It looked like Hilary Clinton was going to win the election. I really felt like she was a carpetbagger and didn't belong here. Stealing a quote from Carol, "I don't believe that the United States Senate should be a consolation prize for a lousy marriage."

As the day endlessly wore on, I became more and more distracted. By the time I reached home, I was in another world. I couldn't find any solace. My mind was racing one minute, and I was practically catatonic the next. The true bi-polar personalities were rearing their ugly heads.

It was about eight in the evening when I spoke to Carol again. The conversation lasted all of ten seconds. Carol whispered in a very compassionate way that she had just gotten off the phone with her mother and Mrs. Parker had heard the rumors a thousand years before and now I knew it was "all true." I don't remember when I hung up.

All I knew was that I knew nothing. My world fell apart in seconds.

My pain was so devastating. There was no consoling me. I don't ever remember crying so much. I just witnessed my own death. The identity that was mine was gone.

My kids were the only people in the world that I truly knew who they were. My whole family was suffering. We were grieving for a life that never was. And Why?

For what reasons?

We didn't know.

Eventually the aches turned to anger.

Diane left, she went straight to Philip's job. She told her Uncle "tell the truth." He responded that he would tell her, but he couldn't tell me. My daughter wouldn't accept that. She demanded that he had to speak to me.

Philip came to the house around midnight. The six of us were petrified of what he was going to say. We wanted to know the answers, but none of us could bear to hear them.

He said that my mother made him and Ceasar swear that they would never tell me of the deep hidden secrets.

He said that he and Ceasar were planning on telling me at Thanksgiving when they could be together. They didn't want the revelations to come out like this. He went on to say this was why my mother kept calling for Ceasar three days before she died. She wanted Ceasar to renew his vow never to tell me.

By this time Philip was crying. I felt pity for my brother, that he was struggling alone to tell me that what Deanna had blurted out was basically the actual story. He said he was told the story when our grandmother died. When he was told, it was made quite clear that it was never going to be spoken of again.

He said he never considered me his half-sister. When I heard him say this, I really went to pieces. My mother was not my mother. I just couldn't grasp what was unfolding? And I still don't.

Wednesday, the next day I tried to work and fell apart there. I returned home. My depression was taking over. I was in bed for days. My physician, Dr. Magun, was extremely sensitive to my pain. He prescribed antidepressants and advised me to seek a psychiatrist's help.

Needless to say, I never attended Victor's funeral. But Philip went, and when he wouldn't speak to Deanna, Aunt Betty called me. I was at the doctor's the first time she called and was relieved I had missed the call. But, then she called again and was very upset that her daughter was treated so shabbily.

Didn't anybody realize I was the victim?

My aunt went on to say she was glad I was seeking help for my depression but she always believed that I had known the story of my birth, that she thought my sister-in-law Joyce told me on my wedding day.

Now things were going from bad to worse, which, given my state of mind, I didn't believe possible. Next my aunt said that maybe I psychologically suppressed it.

The lunacy of what she said was stifling. Why would Joyce tell me such a thing? And why on my Wedding Day?

I never did speak to my uncle. I was so devastated. My whole life had been one lie after another.

Dale called me a few days after Election Day Carol had told her what happened. Dale's mom said that Ernest Innis had somehow heard the story when my grandmother died and told the neighbors that they should not allow their children to play with me, that Virginia was a bastard.

I knew the man despised me and I hated him.

Fortunately, the Parkers and The Greens would not let the vicious man perpetuate more grief for a little girl.

Dale said she didn't find out the story for years. Her mother felt it would have made no difference in our friendship. I always loved Rae Greene.

The truth was that over two hundred people knew the story of my birth and <u>I didn't</u>.

Peter King

I contacted Congressman Peter King's office and spoke to Jason. Jason provided me with the same documentation requirements that I had already received from the passport authority. During this interim, I came to find out that the names I believed to be my parents were in fact not. *Click...* This fact alone was very distressing to me. I informed the passport agency of this problem. I could not obtain any hospital records because Lakeshore Hospital in Copiague, NY burned down in 1971. *Click...* My early school records were destroyed *Click...* and never passed on to my high school in the Bellmore – Merrick Central High School District. The only records that I was able to obtain were my inoculations records. They stated when I was immunized and that I was born in South Nassau Hospital in Oceanside, Long Island. I know that this information is false because it was written by me in my own handwriting. *Click...* One thing you always recognize is your own signature.

Terry and I took a trip back to the Town Hall of Babylon, we acted as if this was the first time we were there. This time the clerk had a different attitude. She turned the book and said there was a child named Virginia born that day in that hospital but as you could see it's not you. I knew it was .Staring me in my face was name of my father, Anthony Demande. A stretch from Philip diMonda, but none the less one and the same. My mother's name was Florence Romano from Boston, Massachusetts.

"Who is she?"

I never heard of her before. How could this woman be my mother?

My Lawyer

When I contacted my own attorney Charlie Rosenblum, I told him I needed to get information from a half century before. I suspected that my grandmother paid someone off to get me into school. I figured she used her lawyer as a liaison or a go between. Before my grandmother died, she appointed Ralph Caso to be my legal guardian, not my own father, *Click...*

But Charlie informed me that Ralph Caso's personal notes were dissolved when he entered public service as the Nassau County Executive. *Click...* My parents never filled out any census report in the 1950s. My parents were never married until May of 1977. They never adopted me. My parents are deceased, their lawyer is deceased. Most of my aunts and uncles are deceased.

January 4, 2001

On January 4, 2001 I went personally to Hudson St. in Manhattan. They didn't want to admit me without an appointment but the agent I spoke to, S. Gayle, informed me I still did not have enough documentation. I explained that there was no more, but I was still denied. Mr. Gayle's Supervisor, Carol, refused to give me her last name, and told me after much discussion, I could have a temporary Passport, good for one year only. At the end of the year I would have to provide more documentation. I cannot produce any more documentation as there is none and there will not be any further information in one year. In fact, in all probability there could be less given the ages and health of the parties concerned Everytime, I comply with the requests made by the Government Offices, they change the demands. The passport authority then asked for an affidavit from each of my relatives and friends. I complied with this request and then they were requesting that I provide proof of these people's statuses. The demands never stopped and I like an obedient child who has been beaten into submission, was forced to conform. All the papers were notarized letters; it didn't matter to the government. *Click...*

I explained that:

"I am a New York City Public High School teacher in Far Rockaway, NY"

No response …

"I have three college degrees; I graduated Magna Cum Laude,"

No response …

Now I have the equivalent of four degrees.

"I ran for public office, to be a commissioner of North Merrick Fire District Commissioner in 1986,"

No response …

"I have never missed an election in 27 years, Local, State, National or Civic."

No response.

I have been called for jury duty several times,"

No response.

I have been very active in North Merrick School District # 29, North Merrick Fire Department and Sacred Heart Church for my entire life, all of which I have lived in North Merrick. My accomplishments and awards could fill up ten letters, yet the government still considers me unfit for a passport. Why? Am I a threat? What have I done to be treated so shabbily?"

Still no response …

I even asked if they thought of me as a terrorist. If I made that remark ten months later, I'm sure I would have been arrested.

As a result of all these distressing happenings, I have been under a doctor's care for the last several years. My question was, "What can my country do for me?" Answer: "Anything they could to compound an already difficult situation." My faith in my elected officials has seriously been questioned. I have asked repeatedly for help, but to no avail. The date the government has set for me to straighten out this matter is January 18, 2001. This date was rapidly approaching and I still had no solution or closure to my exasperating situation. My name is Virginia di Monda McCauley, I was born on October 18, 1944, My SS# is xxx-yy-zzzz I have lived in North Merrick my entire life and have resided at xxxx Gixxxxi Ave. for the past 36 years. My home phone number is (516) xxx –yyyy. After all this frustration, I told my husband I wanted to sue the *Fucking-* government for twenty million dollars. This was just to get someone's attention, so someone would listen.

I had to have some identity; I couldn't go through the rest of my life as a nonentity.

I am someone.

I was someone to begin with.

Now you know why I started this book with my wedding day.

That day I was really Virginia McCauley.

That day I was really a wife.

One year later I was really a mother of a little girl.

Two years later, I was a mother of a son.

Then a mother of a second son and then a mother of a second daughter.

All this I was.

<u>But this was not. all I was</u>.

And nobody was going to take it away from me. Never.

I knew what I was and no one can take it, it's what I am now.

But I had to find out who I was before?

The Only Way

Go public! I decided that I would have to go public with this story. It was the only course left only for me. I E-mailed Ed Lowe, a Newsday reporter. He immediately responded and said he would print my plight. I asked for any assistance he could give me and said it would be greatly appreciated. Mr. Lowe is a very skillful and talented reporter, and he did his research very intensely (so much that because of his inquiry the public article was not needed.)

By the time the article was going to be printed the need for the urgency was gone. I called Ed Lowe and asked him not to print the article.

He said, "No."

I asked him if I could see the article before it went to print.

He said, "No" again.

On Sunday, January 28, 2001, Super bowl Sunday, the piece entitled **Passport to Missing Years and a Secret Life** was printed.

I had originally typed the whole article, word for word, comma for comma. I struggled through tears to which I am not easily moved. It took me hours to type one newspaper page. Checking my spelling and rereading the ordeal forced me to delete the labored reproduction. I could not bear to put the reporter's story in print for a second time.

The fallout from the article was much worse than I could tolerate. It opened the wounds from ten weeks before, wounds that were still raw and burning and hadn't started to close. People called and were curious, some felt I was famous, some expressed compassion and relatives expressed anger and felt I had no right to go public with family business.

Finally we had to take the phone off the hook. My kids were stressed out at their homes and at their jobs. They were ashamed and I was helpless to console them. At Far Rockaway, people made stupid statements like;

"Will you autograph this for me?"

And

"You really don't look 56."

It made me question if that building really had college educated people working at it?

I was living such a bad dream, a nightmare that was getting worse by the moment. The pain was getting excruciating, there was no antidote on hand for me.

Double Play Discovery

Belated Information

On the last day of January 2001 there was an official proclamation of adoption. My Far Rockaway Family, the fifth period lunch group, had a formal luncheon for me. Richard McAuley, was my step-father and Letty Wein. Was my step-mother. Letty was my guiding light from the first day I entered "The Rock."

When I heard from Ed Lowe a few days later, he said that Suffolk County had found something for me.

I knew it was the last document that I had seen; I asked if there was going to be any follow-up stories. He said not unless I wanted them. If I wanted them? It would be like pouring salt on an opened wound.

I politely declined.

Michael Comes to N. Y.

My cousin Mike is the oldest of my Uncle Julie's three children. He is in the Coast Guard Reserve and is the senior chief on the USS Eagle. The Eagle is the United States' Premier Tall Ship; it is used for the training of the freshmen enrolled at the Coast Guard Academy in New London, Connecticut. I hadn't seen Michael in years, but we were camping in Greenport, L.I... The Eagle was anchored in Greenport's harbor. I invited Mike to come to the trailer for dinner. I picked him up and we spoke for a long time. I asked him if he knew about me and when did he find out. He told me his father told him when he questioned why I was the only grandchild to inherit from grandma.

Mike has a quiet demeanor and he said he was told never to discuss the matter and never to reveal it to me, which obviously he never did.

Mike's younger sister, Kathy lived in New York for years. We used to see each other at weddings and funerals, we never communicated other than those occasions .Now she lives in Southern Florida and e-mail her frequently. When my world was falling apart, I spoke to her on the phone and got the same answer as I got from all of my cousins. They knew but were told never to mention it to me. It became a di Monda secret, all about me and hidden as deep as possible.

My cousins on my mother's side never knew anything until the shit hit the fan. Some were resentful that I was treated as a dirty scandal.

9/11 Numb

When you suffer from Bi-Polar Manic Depression, you become so self-absorbed, that the world could fall apart and you wouldn't care.

Well, when the World Trade Center was attacked my only concern was that Brian was in New York City for six days. I know my son will carry that outrageous week within him for the rest of his life. I, like the rest of humanity, was horrified by the terrorists, but I was not confronted by overwhelming grief even though I knew dozens of people who perished. I just became numb to pain of others.

It wasn't that long since my own problems had begun and I still wasn't able to take on anything. My kids had lost personal friends; Brian himself went to more than twenty funerals. Diane had been in the Fire Department in Levittown with a few of them and Amy had worked with one of the guys killed from Merrick. TJ lost school and neighborhood friends. I could see my kids' pain but I couldn't feel it. I felt powerless; I couldn't help them through it. I couldn't shed a tear and it made me ashamed that I reacted so callously.

The following summer, Terry and I went out West to tour the National Parks. After we visited the Grand

Canyon, we went to see Barbara Schrody in Glendale, Arizona; she lives in a suburb of Phoenix.

Barbara was also a friend of my brother; he met her through his fraternity. Barbara's family lived in Roosevelt. Before she got married, she lived at our house on Merrick Ave. and we were become very close. She lived in Merrick and then before they moved out west for Joe to work, Barbara and Joe lived in Merrick with their three little kids. Joe died twenty years ago. Barbara couldn't afford to come back.

New York is like the song *Childhood*, and as the lyrics go:

"Once you leave its borders, you can never return again."

It had been quite a few years since I saw my friend and I was happy to visit. We talked for hours and Barbara revealed that she also knew of my plight. It seems my mother had confided in her mother and again she and her sister were told not to speak to me about it..

The whole incident has changed me immensely. I don't pull the practical jokes anymore. I'm very defensive and I don't trust people. I quickly become combative and confrontational. Most of the humor has gone from my life.

I'm moody and I snap quickly.

Garage Sale

On October 16, 2002, notably my father's birthday, I was going through piles of junk and boxes of knick-knacks. I had to clean up the years of accumulated stuff, stuff, I saved for God knows what reason. As I picked up each piece of memorabilia, I started to reminisce about the how and why I saved this forgotten treasure. This task was arduous and took hours. Terry's patience was waning, but we were having a garage sale the following weekend, and chores had to be done.

When my mother died, I hastily packed her few belongings and brought them back to New York. During my mother's wake my brothers and I divided up her meager treasures. Now, sixteen years later, I was going through my mother's personal things that I had carried from Florida. It was sad to know a whole life of seventy-two years, three children, and ten grandchildren all could fit into one small suitcase. Terry was getting annoyed at how long it was taking me, but I didn't care. I just had to read and inspect every single thing. Time was of the essence, and there I sat at the kitchen table with my mom's address book. I went through the pages one by one, commenting on this person or that relative. By the time I reached the end of the alphabet Terry was about ready to scream.

Suddenly my heart was in my throat. I could barely tell my husband about what I saw. It was staggering and I was really taken back when I came across the name Romano with a lightly penciled X through it. My husband immediately grabbed the Suffolk County phone book to see if the address matched, and there glaring at me, was the name Peter Romano. My Uncle Pressy told me that the woman who gave birth to me was Florence Romano and she already had a son named PETER.

I didn't call the phone number. Maybe by the time I finish this autobiography I will.

I often wonder about this other family. I wonder if I have any resemblance to them. I will eventually have to find out more since they live on Long Island. I don't want my children falling into a relationship, unaware that this partner is their own first cousin that they never knew about.

I have to find out if Florence Romano was or is a Bi-Polar Manic Depressive. This horrible disease is carried generally through the female side of the family. It frightens me...

Uncle Eddie Dies

Deanna's fiancé Richard committed suicide. As distraught as I was with her, I still felt some sympathy for her. I couldn't bring myself to go to the wake but I just couldn't ignore it . I sent my cousin a Mass card with a short note saying I was sorry for her loss.

Three weeks later I received a phone call from D.D.; she called to say her father died. I felt terrible. I never spoke to my Uncle Ed since my troubles began. I don't know why he didn't speak to me or try to help me with the government. I was always the closest to him of all my uncles. When I was growing up, he taught me how to drive; he fixed every lawn mower I ever wrecked. He was always the knight in shining armor next door, but most of all, he was always there. I did a reading at his funeral, except it wasn't the words that should have been spoken the year before.

Philip came to the funeral. I felt he was perplexed with my actions. I had to do something, and that expression was my only alternative.

About a month after my uncle passed away, Aunt Betty invited me to dinner. Diane and Amy were going to come with Terry and me. I was sure the whole incident was going to come up. I didn't want to discuss it. Right before we were all set to leave the house, my cousin Thomas showed up. I immediately invited him to join us and then called my aunt.

I wanted to guarantee what the conversation would be and with Tom there I did.

Uncle Pressy goes to England

Uncle Pressy married a woman named Kay.
Kay is originally from Great Britain. I am delighted that my uncle found a nice woman to be with and enjoy.

Kay's grandson was getting married in England. Well, my uncle needed a passport. So who does he call? Ironic, isn't it? Actually I had the greatest experience with the State Department and the Bureau of Vital Statistics. Guess who got Uncle Pressy the forms to get his birth certificate?

Italy Again

On September 25, 2003, I went to #1 Travel Inc. in Merrick, NY to inquire about a trip to Italy for six people. When I lost the opportunity to go on the faculty trip three years before, my daughters said they would take me, but instead Terry and I gave them the trip as a Christmas present.

I should have checked out the inaccuracies of this company before booking this trip. "Caveat emptor" means " Let the buyer beware.

On February 12, 2004 the day before our departure, I made another call, this time to check on our seats. I expressed my dismay at this agency's service and asked specifically what **This Company** was going to do for me? I was told that they were going to take care of us "that the trip didn't even start yet." How magnanimous of them, <u>it never happened</u>. We arrived at JFK Airport four and a half hours before departure. Delta told us that because we were so early we would be placed **<u>first</u>** on the stand-by as we never got seat assignments from our travel agency. We finally managed to get on the plane two by two, in all different areas of the plane. Coming home the seating was worse and we were the last people on the plane, and only because some servicemen went to Paris via` Alitalia. We also were offered a trip to France, but the Parisian air traffic controllers were on strike and it was snowing there (and then we would have to go to Atlanta, Georgia.) Delta informed us that because we didn't have seat assignments that their only obligation was to get us to the United States within twenty four hours of the departure time. We arrived in Italy on Saturday morning and had a wonderful ride from the airport to the hotel. We then waited three hours for rooms and the elevator didn't work.

Sunday, we all took a taxi and visited the Vatican ourselves. We regrettably didn't wait to see the Pope, but we did attend mass in Saint Peter's. That afternoon we took the train to Ansio, site of the great WW II battle. We got ripped off by the cab driver and were in the wrong town; P.S. the cabbie was gone after getting us for $40.00 to go a few blocks. When we reboarded the train, I asked some teenagers if they spoke English. They mimicked me and made up a phony language in reply. My response to them was to ask if they knew what "Fuck Off" means? They did and sheepishly walked away.

One tour gave us ten minutes in the Sistine Chapel. Big Deal.

February 17, 2004, my brother's 68th birthday, the second tour was to Florence, a beautiful city on a bus without a bathroom. We finally arrived and proceeded on a walking tour. I myself am disabled due to numerous foot surgeries so I found the trip painful and very difficult. Michelangelo's <u>David</u> was unbelievable and the Baptistery doors were magnificent, but the walking was insurmountable. I informed our tour guide, Claudio that we were leaving the trip; we wanted to take the train back (we should have taken the train there..) At this time, I was insulted and told that Americans should learn to walk more and not drive every where they go. Who the hell was he to talk to me like that? and to think we paid over a hundred bucks each for this tour. When I said we were "leaving now!", he convinced me we were going to eat immediately and that the bus to take us back was on the corner. The food was inedible and we were still not sure what it was. But Terry and Ceasar had to eat it or pass out, and then Caesar got sick. He was sick for the next few days. Happy Birthday, Ceasar. The bus around the corner was approximately a mile and a half from the corner. Claudio walked with me trying to help me get to the bus faster. All of a sudden, he was concerned. The next day, inspired only by ourselves, we went to the Coliseum and the Spanish Step and the Pantheon. No stress except when the cab with Diane, Amy and Ceasar hit a bus and everyone kept driving! On Thursday, we were picked up on time and driven to the bus office It was raining horrendously and very cold. We were told when we were on the bus that the trip was even longer than Florence and there was no bathroom. We stated that a few members were sick from the Florence trip, so we would remain on the bus at the Pompeii. I was told that this was not possible as the bus would be leaving and the ruins were a 45 minute walk from the bus drop off. We were told we could get a refund of $492.00 and if we went back into the tour office. They told us to present our receipt to our agency and we would get our refund.

After returning to our hotel rooms soaking wet cold and miserable we tried to recuperate for our trip home, Friday, As I previously explained our flight home was more stressful than the trip to Italy. The plane was filled with people accompanying a group from Chaminade High School. I was sitting with their tour arranger. They had assigned seats and booked their flight and tour in the middle of October 2003, and I booked our trip at the end of September 2003. Why did they get seats and we did not? Am I just a schmuck, that anything that can go wrong usually does? Did they call me? They did not!

After returning home, I placed many phone calls to our wonderful? Agency with never a response.

Finally, on March 11, 2004, I dropped by the Agency. I was told that owner was at an appointment. A lie because a few minutes later not one of the four people in the office knew where she was. No one seemed to know what I was talking about or who I was? But, surprisingly enough, they knew I didn't go to Pompeii because of the rain.. Did they just pull that thought out of a hat?

By this time I was like a raving maniac.

I told them: "You people make Martha Stewart look like Mother Teresa."

They threatened to call the police.

I guess the reason for their attitude was that whenever the phone rang, I would yell and tell people "Hang up, you're going to get taken by these liars." My response to their threat was:

"Go ahead! Call the cops. I will tell them I was robbed."

Then they told me that a letter was written asking about my refund. Another lie .They just wanted me off their premises.

"Can you blame them?"

Lastly, on March 13, 2004, I spoke to the owner, Beverly. After an hour, I found out no letter was written by any one. **I wanted my refund.** I gave my money to #1. I told her it's her obligation for me to be taken care of. I should not have to spend all my time and energy for an Agency that provided nothing but lies, rudeness, and inaccurate information. They never returned phone calls and always had an excuse for a terrible trip being some other party's fault. I kept getting angrier.

I eventually put a small claims case against # 1 Travel; I placed the claim for $5,000.00 Beverly put in for a postponement. Ceasar was going in for a heart cauterization. His heart problems ended with him needing five bypasses.

The tour company decided to settle even though I was going after the travel agency. I didn't have to go back to court. We ended up with a little over a thousand dollars. I just wanted this whole thing over and done with. Afterwards, everytime, I heard from #1 Travel, I would be sick to my stomach.

The Call

On January 4, 2005 at 7:45 PM, I made the call to the number in my mother's address book. There was no answer. I then checked the Suffolk County phone directory and found the street address was different by three numbers. I also discovered that one digit was wrong, it was off by one. The telephone book was four years old; I had found the number two years ago. I should have made the call then, because when I finally had the courage to do the deed, it was too late. The people that answered the phone had no idea about whom I was talking. They said they had that phone number for only six months. I guess any relation to my birth relatives were gone within the last two years. I made several more phone calls but I had no luck. I don't know if it my destiny to never know the secrets hundreds have tried to keep who succeeded.

I chose this date because it was exactly four years since my legendary visit to the State Department in New York City. There is still one slight possibility of another number but, as of this date, no one has answered the phone, and I won't leave this kind of delicate, personal message on an answering machine.

Another Crisis

I was getting prepared to ship out this manuscript. I was having a problem with the e-mail. On the Friday before the Passover break, Ann Spence and I were talking about the snag. School had been dismissed when I received a message from Terry to come home that we had a car parked in our kitchen. He didn't seem too upset and I know that he's easily distressed, so I didn't get worked up over his message. Ann said "Nothing is ever dull at the McCauley house. Now you have to add another chapter."

So here's the scoop. The timing was incredible; it was one week before our fortieth anniversary and just two weeks before Kylie's first birthday.

Karen received a frantic call from our neighbor, Cathy Jarosak. When Karen heard all the sirens and fire engines in the background, she knew there was big trouble. Cathy told Karen, "There's nobody home at your in-law's house and a car had just driven through the side of it."

Karen called TJ!

Who called Amy!

Who called and woke up Diane.

When the fire department got to my house they realized, that Terry, Brian and I were not home. One of

Brian's friends called him on his cell. Brian thought someone was playing a stupid joke when he realized that it wasn't a hoax, he called his father. Terry was on his way home from the store. A few days before, he had received two DVD players for his birthday. He was returning one of them when he got the call from Brian. When he reached the house, he called me at work to come home.

Half of the house was damaged. The kitchen was completely destroyed. Every cabinet was ripped off the wall. The plumbing was twisted into knots like a drunken sailor was trying to hoist a mast in a hurricane. Water was gushing everywhere. The back door was on top of the stove. The counter top and the wall shifted so significantly that you couldn't open the refrigerator door and that's a very serious situation in my family. The appliances suddenly became *Whirlpools*. That would explain them swirling around the kitchen.

The electric was ripped out of the bathroom, when the walls were driven to a new location by a '97 Honda. The medicine cabinet was jarred out of its recess, the ceiling buckled and the fixtures were jolted to different spots.

My lovely garden wall which was just built the year before was scattered across my lawn.

Thank God the dogs escaped injury.

If Terry had been in his usual kitchen chair, he probably wouldn't have survived.

Everyone proclaimed that we were all so lucky.

To me, Lucky is not having a car drive through your

house.

We were supposed to go to Ceasar's.

That trip was cancelled as well as the summer ones.

The trailer became our living quarters.

And the battle began.

Everywhere you looked was like downtown Baghdad.

I'm already fighting for control of my stress.

Tribute to My Mother – My Real Mother

I only had one mother. Some stranger gave birth to me. But my mother gave me life. My mother! I am starting to figure out the rationale behind my mother's actions. I realize all the sacrifices she made for a child that was never hers, a child she loved so dearly that she would go to any lengths to protect. A child who made her live with guilt for over half of her life. A guilt that was never hers to begin with. A pure love that she gave and that she never had fully returned to her.

September, 8th is the birthday of Mary, the mother of Jesus. My mother's birthday was September 10th. Mary died and ascended into heaven on August 15th . My mother died and went to heaven on August 15th. Lives that were so parallel are truly blessed. Two women who raised and loved a child that they were commanded to. Two women who were not expecting the birth of that child to change them for the rest of their own lives.

Please don't think in anyway that I am comparing myself to Jesus. But I am in every way comparing my mother to Mary.

My mother was told to raise me, she and my dad were not legally married. All of a sudden she takes me and my brothers and runs to Brooklyn.

She wasn't running to safety, she was running to shelter, to the shelter of her own parents.

She took me, a child she had no claim to, a child she had no right to.

A child whom she knew could only cause her grief.

Why did she do what she did?

I can only guess that she wanted to love a little girl, and, she was going to, no matter what the consequences. She was going to jump from the frying pan into the fire, not caring how much she would get burned.

When she appeared at my grandparents' house, they insisted on me being baptized immediately. Thus, my godparents are my mother's brother, Dan and her sister, Dolly. Ceasar, Philip, Mommy and I stayed in Bay Ridge until her mother was killed. She tragically fell down the steps while moving laundry to the roof. I was very young and my recollection of living in the city is especially vague. I never really existed legally; my family did what they had to do to keep their secret. I never received any medical attention, I never had any inoculations, and my broken leg was never tended to. I never had any school pictures taken. I didn't legally live until I was married.

A teenage girl is such a challenge and I was such a bitch. She didn't have to put up with me. My grandma had died a few years before, yet she continued to give love and take abuse from me and my father. I believed he truly loved her and me. I know she loved him so much that she suffered his indiscretions for over forty years.

As for me, she had to have had such a great love that she never had returned to her. I always resented the estranged relationship, a divided relationship that was never peaceful.

I take exception to the fact that no one ever trusted me enough to know the truth and no one ever gave me the opportunity to return the love that I should have. I feel cheated and guilty. I don't hold blame, but my life has changed dramatically. My sense of humor is just a small fraction of what it was. I lost my trust in people.

But what I regret the most is I never told my mother, "I love you." God knows she loved me and she took that love with her secret sixteen years after she died.

I know its sixty years late, "I love you, Mom."

And Life Continues. *Click...*